PRESS THROUGH FOR BREAKTHROUGH

Trust your Father God through it all

LIZ ROBINSON

↑ SPIRIT-LED
⇞ PUBLISHING

Press Through for Breakthrough: Trust your Father God through it all

Copyright © 2019 by Liz Robinson.

All rights reserved. No part of this publication may be reproduced, distributed or transmitted in any form or by any means, including photocopying, recording, or other electronic or mechanical methods, without the prior written permission of the publisher, except in the case of brief quotations embodied in critical reviews and certain other noncommercial uses permitted by copyright law. For permission requests, write to the author at the e-mail address below.

liz@coachmybusiness.com

Unless otherwise indicated, all Scripture is taken from the New King James Version®. Copyright © 1982 by Thomas Nelson. Used by permission. All rights reserved.

All Scripture quotations marked NIV are taken from the HOLY BIBLE, NEW INTERNATIONAL VERSION®. NIV®. Copyright © 1973, 1978, 1984 by International Bible Society. Used by permission of Zondervan. All rights reserved worldwide.

All Scripture quotations marked GNB are taken from the Good News Bible © 1994 published by the Bible Societies/HarperCollins Publishers Ltd UK, Good News Bible© American Bible Society 1966, 1971, 1976, 1992. Used with permission.

All Scripture quotations marked HNV are taken from the Hebrew Names Version of the World English Bible, a modern English update of the American Standard Version. This translation is in the public domain.

All Scripture quotations marked AMP are taken from the Amplified® Bible. Copyright © 2015 by The Lockman Foundation. Used by permission. www.Lockman.org.

All Scripture quotations marked NLT are taken from the Holy Bible, New Living Translation, copyright ©1996, 2004, 2015 by Tyndale House Foundation. Used by permission of Tyndale House Publishers, Inc., Carol Stream, Illinois 60188. All rights reserved.

All Scripture quotations marked KJV are taken from the King James Bible, which is in the public domain.

Editing, typesetting, and cover design: Sally Hanan of Inksnatcher.com
Cover photo: https://www.123rf.com/profile_lilkar

Ordering Information:
Quantity sales. Special discounts are available on quantity purchases by corporations, associations, and others. For details, contact the author at the e-mail address above.

Press Through for Breakthrough: Trust your Father God through it all/Liz Robinson
ISBN 9781943011087

This book is dedicated to Father God, Jesus Christ His Son, and Holy Spirit for leading and guiding me in writing this book. Thank you, Charles and Nathanael, for your love and encouragement to me and interest in this book.

CONTENTS

I. God's Breakthrough

1. God's Pressing for Breakthrough — 1
2. God's Anointing for Breakthrough — 9
3. God's Zeal for Breakthrough — 19
4. God's Authority for Breakthrough — 29
5. God's Words for Breakthrough — 37

II. Your Breakthrough

6. Pursue God for Breakthrough — 47
7. Rest in God — 65
8. Emulate Jesus for Breakthrough — 85
9. Sensitize Yourself to Holy Spirit — 99
10. Stand Firm in Christ — 121

III. Biblical Breakthrough

11. Bible Heroes Pressed Through — 135
12. Kings, Judges, and Prophets Pressed Through — 145

Appendices A–G — 163

About the Author — 179

Letter from Liz

Dear reader,

My heart's desire is that this book will help you to press through for breakthrough, and I hope it will help you to become even closer to God and His Word.

In *Press Through for Breakthrough* I present key principles and Scriptures that have transformed my life and helped me to achieve breakthrough. I hope this book will do the same for you and that the Lord will give you even deeper revelation on the topics I present. He loves you so much, and He is excited for you to know Him more!

May you embrace the process of pressing through and seeing your breakthrough come forth!

Liz Robinson

OF NOTE

I predominantly use the New King James Version (NKJV) for Scriptures and do not notate when this is done, unless I am using it in comparison with another version. However, when I include the New International Version (NIV), Hebrew Names Version (HNV), and Amplified Version (AMP), I notate this after the Scripture.

Sometimes I use the term "enemy" for the devil and Satan. Jesus speaks about the devil and Satan in these Scriptures: John 8:44, Matthew 4:1, 10

For the sake of not repeating the names of God the Father, Jesus Christ, His Son, and Holy Spirit, at times I will refer to each of them as God, the Lord God, or the Lord. However, when Scripture states what God the Father, Jesus, and Holy Spirit say and do, I will state this, as it helps you to learn more about them individually and their function.

Liz Robinson

Acknowledgments

This book is based on my first message I wrote and taught to the body of Christ on how to press through for breakthrough. As I searched Scripture for the meaning of words in Hebrew and Greek, I enjoyed seeing how they confirmed God's intense desire to give us breakthrough and each other. This book is also about the ways I needed to surrender to my heavenly Father, Jesus, and Holy Spirit and learn life-giving principles in God's Word. When I applied these to my life, I gained understanding of His ways and freedom to rise above the cares of this world. My desire is to share this with you so you will have breakthrough too.

I thank my dear husband, Charles, who lovingly and consistently cheered me on, showed confidence in my writing, and told me how this book will be helpful to many. I thank my dear son, Nathanael, for seeing my love of research and encouraging me in so many ways, and who patiently listened as I read parts of my book to him.

I thank my dear friend and mentor, Jim Walter, Th.M. Executive Director for the Center for Relational Care in Austin, TX, for being a life support to me in my walk with God when I was learning how to press through for breakthrough. His love, care, dedication, and ability to apply God's Word to my situations dramatically gave me insight, strength, and courage to hope, grow, and flourish in my faith.

I thank my dear pastors Dr. George W. Walters, Jr., Senior Pastor and President of Faith Theological Seminary and Christian College and Dr. Mickey L. Walters in Tampa, FL. They taught me foundations on how to live the Christian life, develop a close relationship with the Lord, serve the local church, and serve our pastors. They also taught me how to serve those who do not know him yet, and my brothers and sisters in Christ, through love, evangelism, studying, applying God's Word, and so much more.

I am very appreciative for pastors Mickey Freed and Dr. Sandy Freed of Life Gate Church International in Hurst, TX, who lovingly trained and mentored me in the gifts of the Spirit and believed in me and submitted me for licensure and ordination through Christian International Ministries. Additionally, I am very thankful to them for overseeing my husband and me as we pastored a local church in Austin, TX. I am very grateful to Dr. Bill Hamon of Christian International Ministries for licensing and ordaining me and for being a great blessing to me and my family.

I am very grateful to my friend Nicholas Sanchez for his joy, interest, and encouragement to me on how to pace myself well in writing and finishing this book.

I would like to acknowledge with gratitude the support and love of other family and friends who shared excitement and interest in this book.

I am very thankful for my editor, Sally Hanan, for helping me bring forth my ideas in a smooth and succinct way. She helped me weave together the sections of my book to create a beautiful tapestry.

I am very appreciative to the commentators and resources I referenced for their wisdom and insight into God's Word.

I. God's Breakthrough

— 1 —

God's Pressing for Breakthrough

MATTHEW 26:39

> *O My Father, if it is possible, let this cup pass from Me.*

Are you pressing into God to receive your breakthrough? Are you also allowing God to press upon your life to receive your breakthrough? When God presses into your life, He does so with His great love and compassion for you. He wants to bring forth the best in your life! His pressing process is a good one because it brings you good change, transformation, and new life in Him.

The Old Testament gives us an excellent allegory of what God's pressing looks like, through the function of the olive press. The Israelites used an olive press, a huge stone that rolled over olives, to release their valuable oil. We are like the olive, and God desires that you allow the pressing circumstances in your life to bring forth His oil of gladness and anointing (empowerment) for your breakthrough.

God's Pressing for Breakthrough

Ancient olive press

Olive oil and the Holy Spirit

Olive oil is produced through a pressing method. The olives are ground, and the paste is then spread onto disks which are stacked into a column before being placed into the press. Pressure is then applied onto the column to separate the oil from the paste.

Olive oil was, and is, mostly used for cooking and for fuel for traditional oil lamps. The first recorded oil extraction was mentioned in the Hebrew Bible and took place during the thirteenth century BC, when the Israelites fled Egypt, so to this day it holds special significance in Jewish culture.

> In Jewish observance, olive oil was the only fuel allowed to be used in the seven- branched Menorah in the Mishkan service during the Exodus of the tribes of Israel from Egypt, and later in the permanent temple in Jerusalem. It was obtained by using only the first drop from a squeezed olive and was consecrated for use only in the temple by the priests and stored in special containers.
>
> . . .
>
> Another use of oil in Jewish religion is for anointing the kings of the Kingdom of Israel, originating from King

David. . . . Olive oil mixed with a perfuming agent such as balsam . . . is used . . . in . . . the ordination of priests and bishops, in the consecration of altars and churches, and, traditionally, in the anointing of monarchs at their coronation.[1]

Just as the Israelites used the olive press to press olives—to get the valuable oil for food, light, and more—so is your heavenly Father God going to use your pressing to bring forth the valuable oil of His Holy Spirit. The rich olive oil represents God's power, love, and breakthrough in your life. This oil will flow through your life to bless you and others.

JESUS WAS PRESSED IN THE GARDEN OF GETHSEMANE

Jesus knew that the outcome of Father God's pressing on the final portion of His life would change history. He trusted in and willingly surrendered to His Father's pressing to bring forth the rich oil from His life—oil that was needed to bring salvation, cleansing, healing, comfort, light, and anointing for empowerment and consecration to a lost and dying world.

I was in the garden of Gethsemane in Israel a few years ago, and it was such a peaceful place to reflect on what the Lord Jesus went through during His time there, before His arrest. The word *gethsemane* means "an oil press," so in the garden of Gethsemane Jesus went through a tremendous pressing in the "garden of the oil press."[2] His pressing was much like that of an olive in an olive press, with the goal of releasing the rich oil and anointing of the Holy Spirit to endure what lay ahead in His trial, scourging, and crucifixion. In that place of pressing, with Father God, Jesus pressed through for breakthrough. He was willing to do God's will by going to the cross to redeem all of mankind.

Then Jesus came with them to a place called Gethsemane, and said to the disciples, "Sit here while I go and pray over

> there." And He ... began to be sorrowful and deeply distressed.... He went a little farther and fell on His face, and prayed, saying, "O My Father, if it is possible, let this cup pass from Me; nevertheless, not as I will, but as You will." ... Again, a second time, He went away and prayed, saying, "O My Father, if this cup cannot pass away from Me unless I drink it, Your will be done." And He ... went away again, and prayed the third time, saying the same words."
>
> — Matthew 26:36, 37, 39, 42–44

Jesus felt the pressing and pressure so intensely that Luke stated, "Then His sweat became like great drops of blood falling down to the ground" (Luke 22:43–44). This is a condition called hematidrosis, "a condition in which capillary blood vessels that feed the sweat glands rupture, causing them to exude blood, occurring under conditions of extreme physical or emotional stress. Severe mental anxiety activates the sympathetic nervous system to invoke the stress fight-or-flight response to such a degree as to cause hemorrhage of the vessels supplying the sweat glands into the ducts of the sweat glands."[3]

I don't believe I've heard of anyone I know going through so much pressing that they have sweated blood, but the condition proves the distress Jesus went through as He endured His pressing. Jesus went through many pressing times in His life on earth, but His time in the garden of Gethsemane, when He surrendered His will to Father God's will to go to the cross, was surely very difficult.

You Can Trust Him Through Your Pressing

Jesus knows what it is like for you to go through pressing times, and He is with you and encouraging you every step of the way, so hold on to Him and press through for your breakthrough.

God's Pressing for Breakthrough

Maybe you feel God's "press" in your relationships or finances or in your need for healing and deliverance from old mind-sets, opinions, and behaviors. If you are feeling His press upon your life for good change, I encourage you that He is loving and faithful to bring you victory and breakthrough!

> SAY WITH ME, I'M PRESSING THROUGH FOR MY BREAKTHROUGH!

At times, the hardest part of your pressing is trusting your Father God. Know that God knows the beginning from the end: "He has made everything beautiful in its time. Also He has put eternity in their hearts, except that no one can find out the work that God does from beginning to end" (Ecclesiastes 3:11). He is intimately involved in the details of your life, and He cares about you very much. He knows you better than you know yourself, for He created you. He can see what you cannot see. He knows what you do not know about circumstances, people, and other things. His thoughts are higher than your thoughts: "'For My thoughts are not your thoughts, nor are your ways My ways,' says the Lord. 'For as the heavens are higher than the earth, so are My ways higher than your ways, and My thoughts than your thoughts'" (Isaiah 55:8–9). Will you trust Him to lead you as He presses in your life to bring you good, healthy change, even when you may not understand it?

IN THE VALLEY

Gethsemane, where the garden of Gethsemane lay, is a very plentiful valley at the foot of the Mount of Olives beyond the Kidron Valley—the valley on the eastern side of the Old City of Jerusalem, separating the Temple Mount from the Mount of Olives.[4,5] It was about one-half or three-quarters of an English mile from the walls of Jerusalem, and one hundred yards east of the bridge over the Kedron (*Kidron*).[6] You may have heard it said that you go down to valleys and up to mountaintops in your life, and that the valleys represent challenging times. Your Lord Jesus was in the valley in the garden of Gethsemane, and He knows what it is like for you to be in the valley of sadness, stress, pain, and confusion. He is with you in every valley, and you are never alone. And when you receive Jesus as your Lord and Savior, He teaches you many important things in each valley about Himself, life, and the importance of your relationship with Him.

The Lord is always with you in the challenges of your life, and He wants to give you breakthrough. He is cheering you on to victory! Sometimes He will press into your life by calling you out of something that may not be the best for you—something physically, emotionally, mentally, spiritually, financially, morally, relationally, or socially unhealthy for you. He wants to protect you and give you His best. He wants to keep you from harm. He upholds you in the valley and helps you to press through for breakthrough. He teaches you to trust in Him and to follow Him. He also brings you out of your valleys and takes you up to new heights—to the mountaintops—to see and experience beautiful vistas with Him.

God is very efficient, and He is the great multiplier. Just like there are many uses for olive oil—made from pressing the olives—He wants to make the most use out of your pressing into Him and His pressing process in your life. He wants to give you great breakthrough! He wants to bring forth cleansing, healing, comfort, light, anointing (for empowerment), and consecration (for service) in your life. He wants to enrich your life in wonderful ways.

Ask yourself:

— Will I, like Jesus, surrender my will to His during my hard times and trust Him with the outcome?

NOTES

[1] Olive Oil: https://en.wikipedia.org/wiki/Olive_oil.

[2] https://www.blueletterbible.org/lang/lexicon/lexicon.cfm?Strongs=G1068&t=NKJV.

[3] Hematidrosis: https://en.wikipedia.org/wiki/Hematidrosis.

[4] Hitchcock, R. "Gethsemane – Hitchcock's Bible Names Dictionary." Blue Letter Bible. Last Modified 24 Jun, 1996. https://www.blueletterbible.org/search/Dictionary/viewTopic.cfm.

[5] Kidron Valley: https://en.wikipedia.org/wiki/Kidron_Valley.

[6] Smith, W. "Gethsemane - Smith's Bible Dictionary." Blue Letter Bible. Last Modified 14 Dec, 2010. https://www.blueletterbible.org/search/Dictionary/viewTopic.cfm.

— 2 —
God's Anointing for Breakthrough

1 JOHN 2:27–28

> *The anointing which you have received from Him abides in you, . . . And now, little children, abide in Him.*

The Bible is full of rich symbolism, especially when talking about the oil of the Holy Spirit.

ANOINTING AND ABUNDANCE

> The olive tree has been thought of as a symbol of peace, ever since the dove sent out by Noah from the ark came back, and "Lo, in her mouth an olive leaf plucked off" (Genesis 8:11).
>
> Throughout the Bible, oil is often used symbolically of the HOLY SPIRIT. And when the Apostle John speaks of the "anointing which ye have received" (I John 2:27), he means by it the enduement with power of the HOLY SPIRIT. Also oil was considered a symbol of abundance (Deuteronomy 8:8), and a lack of it was a symbol of want (Joel 1:10).
>
> — Fred H. Wight, *Manners and Customs of Bible Lands*[1]

The Lord God wants to anoint you with His rich oil—His abundance—from the olive tree of peace. God anoints you with His Holy Spirit, who empowers you to do many things—preach, teach, sing, play instruments, write, act, draw, paint, and so much more. You can feel God's presence through His Holy Spirit with you and in you as He anoints (empowers) you. You can also see, hear, and feel Holy Spirit's anointing on others when they operate in their gifts and callings.

> Spiritual anointing with the Holy Ghost is conferred also upon Christians by God 2 Co 1:21 "Anointing" expresses the sanctifying influences of the Holy Spirit upon Christians who are priests and kings unto God.[2]

ANOINTED AND EMPOWERED

The exact translation for *anointing* in many parts of the Bible is "to rub with oil, to paint, to consecrate, to anoint," and olive oil was the primary oil available.[3] Today, oil is still used as a symbol for God's anointing (empowerment). The Lord your God, Jesus, and Holy Spirit consecrate and sanctify you for service in ministry, healing, and more. You do not need to be literally anointed with oil to be anointed by the Holy Spirit. When you receive Jesus as your Lord and Savior, you are His, and His Holy Spirit lives in you. However, you can—through an act of faith and as a prophetic act—anoint yourself with oil to symbolize healing, consecration, devotion, and service to the Lord your God, or have a fellow believer in Christ or elder of the church anoint you for healing and service.

ANOINTED, CONSECRATED, AND SANCTIFIED

Olive oil was also used to consecrate or sanctify people and things. By participating in this process, they were prepared, dedicated, made holy, set apart, honored, pronounced sacred, made clean (ceremonially or morally), or kept holy and purified.⁴ Consecration is important to God. He called for people and articles in the tabernacle of meeting to be anointed with oil: "So I will consecrate the tabernacle of meeting and the altar. I will also consecrate both Aaron and his sons to minister to Me as priests" (Exodus 29:44). Additional examples of anointing are when the prophet Samuel anointed David as king (1 Samuel 16:13) and the priest Zadok anointed David's son Solomon as king (1 Kings 1:39). This symbolized anointing, consecration, and sanctification of God's blessing and calling on people's lives for specific purposes and service—such as a priest, king, and prophet—as well as for preparation for burial and healing.

> For He delivered us and saved us and called us with a holy calling [a calling that leads to a consecrated life—a life set apart—a life of purpose], not because of our works [or because of any personal merit—we could do nothing to earn this], but because of His own purpose and grace [His amazing, undeserved favor] which was granted to us in Christ Jesus before the world began [eternal ages ago].
>
> — 2 Timothy 1:9 AMP

The Lord your God anoints you, consecrates you, and sanctifies you. He prepares you and dedicates you. He asks you to be holy and separate; He sets you apart to be honored and treated as sacred. He makes you clean and pronounces that you are clean, ceremonially and morally, and He purifies you. He sets you apart to serve Him and live for Him when you receive Jesus as your Lord and Savior by faith.

It is important to note that you receive these blessings by having faith in Him. Everything that you receive from God and in the kingdom of God is by faith. It is all received by faith. It's not received by a material possession, a written contract, or anything tangible in the natural physical realm. It is by faith. (Please see Appendix A, "Characteristics of Faith.")

ANOINTED FOR HEALING

In the Bible, a woman anointed Jesus's body for His burial (Mark 14:3-9), and elders of the church anointed people for healing:

> Is anyone among you suffering? Let him pray. Is anyone cheerful? Let him sing psalms. Is anyone among you sick? Let him call for the elders of the church, and let them pray over him, anointing him with oil in the name of the Lord. And the prayer of faith will save the sick, and the Lord will raise him up. And if he has committed sins, he will be forgiven. Confess your trespasses to one another, and pray for one another, that you may be healed.
>
> — James 5:13-16

ANOINTED WITH JOY

God also anoints and empowers us with His joy: "God, your God, has set you above your companions by anointing you with the oil of joy" (Psalm 45:7 NIV). In other words, God rubs with oil, consecrates, or paints us with joy![5] Like the olive press that presses on the olives to release rich oil, Jesus pressed into Father God and allowed God's pressing process in His life so all mankind could receive the oil of joy! He surrendered His will to Father God's will to release the rich oil of His Holy Spirit in your life to supernaturally empower you to press through for breakthrough!

Jesus's joy was in knowing that when He endured the pressing of God in the garden of Gethsemane and in His suffering, death, and resurrection, He would take away the sins of the world once and for all. "Jesus, the author and finisher of our faith, who for the joy that was set before Him endured the cross, despising the shame" (Hebrews 12:2). He would make salvation available to all mankind.

Jesus gives you His joy, which gives you strength! He knew that by dying for your sins, Father God would send His Holy Spirit, as Jesus's representative, to earth to live in people who receive Him as their Lord and Savior. "'This day is holy to our Lord. Do not sorrow, for the joy of the Lord is your strength'" (Nehemiah 8:10).

SURRENDER BRINGS THE ANOINTING

God so wants to release the rich oil of His Holy Spirit, the Helper (the Spirit of truth), into each person's life. Jesus knew that dying and going to heaven was the best and most efficient way for Him to multiply His ability to be with every single person on the earth at the same time. He did not want you to be left alone when He went to heaven, for He is Immanuel (God with us) through His Holy Spirit in the earth. Jesus knew that Holy Spirit would empower you and bring you freedom, breakthrough, and fulfillment in your relationship with Him, Father God, and Holy Spirit.

> He will give you another Helper, that He may abide with you forever— the Spirit of truth, whom the world cannot receive, because it neither sees Him nor knows Him; but you know Him, for He dwells with you and will be in you. I will not leave you orphans; I will come to you. . . . The Helper, the Holy Spirit, whom the Father will send in My name, He will teach you all things, and bring to your remembrance all things that I said to you. . . . When He, the Spirit of truth, has come, He will guide you into all truth; for He will not speak on His own *authority*, but whatever He hears He will speak; and He will tell you things to come.
>
> — John 14:16–18, 26; 16:13; emphasis mine

The Lord your God wants you to know that as you go through pressing times, He is always with you because His Holy Spirit lives in you! He wants you to have joy in your life, and He anoints you with His joy and strength for breakthrough! Jesus had joy in what was set before Him, and this helped Him to endure the cross.

Though it was excruciatingly difficult for Jesus to go through the pressing process, He chose to do it, with joy, for you. He wants you to know that as you go through hard pressing times, His Holy Spirit, the Spirit of truth, is always with you: "But if the Spirit of Him who raised Jesus from the dead dwells in you, He who raised Christ from the dead will also give life to your mortal bodies through His Spirit who dwells in you" (Romans 8:11).

PRESSING THROUGH KEEPS YOU IN THE ANOINTING

> We are hard-pressed on every side, yet not crushed; we are perplexed, but not in despair; persecuted, but not forsaken; struck down, but not destroyed.
>
> — 2 Corinthians 4:8–9

> The Spirit Himself bears witness with our spirit that we are children of God, and if children, then heirs—heirs of God and joint heirs with Christ, if indeed we suffer with Him, that we may also be glorified together.
>
> For I consider that the sufferings of this present time are not worthy to be compared with the glory which shall be revealed in us.
>
> — Romans 8:16–18

The "glory which shall be revealed in you" is God's magnificence, excellence, preeminence, dignity, and grace.[6] The Lord Jesus seeks and pursues the lost and those who know Him. He wants you to develop a close relationship with Him. When I got saved after reading a salvation message in the back of a book,

God gave me great freedom from strongholds that had kept me in fear. But after this I was not discipled and did not attend a church, so I fell away from the Lord. I was prime picking for the enemy to come in and deceive me and draw me away from Him. Sometime later, I could feel the deep, loving presence of the Holy Spirit wooing me to Him. I could feel His heavy presence around me, pressing upon me and drawing me to leave the darkness and come back into the Lord's glorious light. He wanted me to surrender my will to His will. I decided to press in and receive all that He was giving to me. I wanted to know Him and have fellowship with Him and never be away from Him again. So I responded with a yes and gave my life back to Jesus Christ. I followed Him and learned from Him and others, and I have not looked back again. "For the Son of Man has come to seek and to save that which was lost" (Luke 19:10).

God will bring you joy out of your difficulty and sorrow. He will reward you for pursuing Him and following Him. He is faithful, and He loves you dearly. His Holy Spirit lives in you, anoints you, empowers you, consecrates you, and sanctifies you. "But the anointing which you have received from Him abides in you" (1 John 2:27). He helps you to follow the Lord's will. The Lord asks you to love Him, abide in Him—the true vine—and to live according to His Word so you can have an abundant life of victory, joy, and breakthrough.

Live an anointed, consecrated, and sanctified life with Him, and He will give greatly to you—pressed down, shaken together, and running over, like oil from the olive press. "Give, and it will be given to you: good measure, pressed down, shaken together, and running over will be put into your bosom. For with the same measure that you use, it will be measured back to you" (Luke 6:38). The Lord your God anoints you and brings you joy and breakthrough because He loves you with an everlasting love. "Yes,

I have loved you with an everlasting love; therefore with lovingkindness I have drawn you" (Jeremiah 31:3).

Ask yourself:

- Will I let Him anoint me daily with His Holy Spirit?
- Will I let Him flow through me and minister His oil to others?
- Will I allow Him to consecrate me to His service and sanctify me?
- Will I surrender daily to His will?
- Will I ask Him to empower me in pressing times?
- Will I choose to believe that He will give me breakthrough?
- Will I keep pressing through, in faith?

NOTES

[1] Fred H. Wight, "Olive and Fig Tree Culture," in *Manner and Customs of Bible Lands* (Minneapolis: Billy Graham Evangelistic Association, 1994), ch. 21.

[2] "Anointing." Smith's Bible Dictionary. Accessed March 23, 2018. http://www.bible-history.com/smiths/A/Anointing.

[3] "G1637 - elaion – Strong's Greek Lexicon (NKJV)." Blue Letter Bible. Accessed 13 Mar, 2018. https://www.blueletterbible.org//lang/lexicon/lexicon.cfm?Strongs=G1637&t=NKJV.

[4] "H6942 - qadash – Strong's Hebrew Lexicon (NIV)." Blue Letter Bible. Accessed 13 Mar, 2018. https://www.blueletterbible.org//lang/lexicon/lexicon.cfm?Strongs=H6942&t=NIV.

[5] "H4886 - mashach – Strong's Hebrew Lexicon (NKJV)." Blue Letter Bible. Accessed 13 Mar, 2018. https://www.blueletterbible.org//lang/lexicon/lexicon.cfm?Strongs=H4886&t=NKJV.

[6] "G1391 - doxa - Strong's Greek Lexicon (NKJV)." Blue Letter Bible. Accessed 13 Mar, 2018. https://www.blueletterbible.org//lang/lexicon/lexicon.cfm?Strongs=G1391&t=NKJV.

— 3 —

God's Zeal for Breakthrough

MATTHEW 7:7-8

Ask, and it will be given to you; seek, and you will find; knock, and it will be opened to you. For everyone who asks receives, and he who seeks finds, and to him who knocks it will be opened.

As the Son of Man, Jesus Christ was the perfect embodiment of heaven on earth and of what it looks like to be anointed with the oil of Holy Spirit. He expected people to press into that to receive it. Dr William Smith said the following about anointing in *Smith's Bible Dictionary:*

> In the Old Testament a Deliverer is promised under the title of Messiah, or Anointed, Ps 2:2; Da 9:25,26 and the nature of his anointing is described to be spiritual, with the Holy Ghost. Isa 61:1 see Luke 4:18 In the New Testament Jesus of Nazareth is shown to be the Messiah, or Christ or Anointed, of the Old Testament, Joh 1:41; Ac 9:22; 17:2,3; 18:4,28 and the historical fact of his being anointed with the Holy Ghost is asserted and recorded. Joh 1:32,33; Ac 4:27; 10:38 Christ was anointed as prophet priest and king. [*sic*].[1]

Desperate for Healing

A hemorrhaging woman *pressed* in with the crowd to touch Jesus. She must have believed in Him as the Messiah, Anointed One, Prophet, Priest, and King. She had faith in His anointing:

> And suddenly, a woman who had a flow of blood for twelve years came from behind and touched the hem of His garment. For she said to herself, "If only I may touch His garment, I shall be made well." But Jesus turned around, and when He saw her He said, "Be of good cheer, daughter; your faith has made you well." And the woman was made well from that hour.
>
> — Matthew 9:20–22

> So it was, when Jesus returned, that the multitude welcomed Him, for they were all waiting for Him. . . . But as He went, the multitudes thronged Him. Now a woman, having a flow of blood for twelve years, who had spent all her livelihood on physicians and could not be healed by any, came from behind and touched the border of His garment. And immediately her flow of blood stopped. And Jesus said, "Who touched Me?" When all denied it, Peter and those with him said, "Master, the multitudes throng and *press You*, and You say, 'Who touched Me?'" But Jesus said, "Somebody touched Me, for I perceived *power* going out from Me."
>
> — Luke 8:40,42–46, emphasis mine

The word *press* in the verse above means "to press on all sides, squeeze, press hard." It's the same word used to describe the pressing out of grapes and olives.[2] The woman was desperate, and she was determined to receive everything heaven had to offer. When you are in pressing times of your life and you press through for breakthrough, press in to touch Jesus. Reach in to receive His healing power.

The New King James Version and the King James Version differ on their translations of Luke 8:46, quoted above: "But Jesus said, 'Somebody touched Me, for I perceived power going out from Me'" (NKJV) and "Jesus said, 'Somebody hath touched me: for I perceive that virtue is gone out of me'" (KJV). The King James word *virtue* (for power) here denotes the same thing. When you pursue, reach out, and touch Jesus, He gives you "excellence of soul" (mind, will, and emotions), "power and influence which belong to riches and wealth," "miraculous power," "strength," and "mighty (wonderful) work."[3] Ask of Him, seek Him, and He will answer you and give you breakthrough. "Ask, and it will be given to you; seek, and you will find; knock, and it will be opened to you. For everyone who asks receives, and he who seeks finds, and to him who knocks it will be opened" (Matthew 7:7-8).

The effects of your difficult season can feel like you are being pressed on all sides, squeezed, pressed hard, and going through the pressing out process, like a grape or an olive. But the Lord your God is with you in the pressing process, and when you press in to Him, He will give you all you need.

PRESS IN ZEALOUSLY

We can press in zealously. "The law and the prophets were until John. Since that time the kingdom of God has been preached, and everyone is *pressing* into it" (Luke 16:16, emphasis mine). The word *pressing* here means "to use or apply force," to suffer violence; and "a share in the heavenly kingdom is sought for with the most ardent zeal and the most intense exertion."[4]

To suffer violence also appears later in Matthew: "And from the days of John the Baptist until now the kingdom of heaven suffereth violence, and the violent take it by force" (Matthew 11:12

KJV). *Suffereth violence* in this context means much the same thing: to use or apply force, to press; and "a share in the heavenly kingdom is sought for with the most ardent zeal and the most intense exertion." A person plans "to get a share in the kingdom of God by the utmost earnestness and effort."[5]

The violent who take the kingdom of heaven by force are the strong, forceful, energetic; they "strive to obtain its privileges with the utmost eagerness and effort."[6] The woman who had been bleeding for twelve years pressed through the crowd determinedly, not stopping until she was close enough to touch Jesus's robe. She knew where her healing lay. The Lord wants you to press in like that—to be strong, forceful, energetic; to seek His heavenly kingdom with the most ardent zeal and the most intense exertion, and to strive to obtain the privileges of the kingdom of God with the utmost eagerness and effort.

He will preserve you

When you press through for breakthrough, He preserves you and keeps you safe. He keeps you strong as you stay close to Him and press in to know Him more. He instructs you and teaches you in the way that you should go.

Jesus cares so much for you. He brings you peace. All things were created through Jesus and for Jesus. He keeps everything together in your life, in the world, and in the universe. He is before all things, in Him all things consist, and in Him all fullness dwells. He's got this:

> He is the image of the invisible God, the firstborn over all creation. For by Him all things were created that are in heaven and that are on earth, visible and invisible, whether thrones or dominions or principalities or powers. All things were created through Him and for Him. And He is before all things, and in Him all things consist. . . .

For it pleased the Father that in Him all the fullness should dwell.

— Colossians 1:15–17, 19

Pressing into God while going through pressing times in your life can feel like too much at times. But He will give you breakthrough, protect you, and *preserve* you through it all. "You are my hiding place; you shall preserve me from trouble; you shall surround me with songs of deliverance. *Selah*" (Psalm 32:7). He will sustain you, maintain you, keep you safe from harm, and prepare you for good things to come.

The word *preserve* in the verse above means "to keep safe from injury, harm, or destruction: [to] protect."[7] Joseph, in the Old Testament, said this to his brothers, who sold him into slavery: "But now, do not therefore be grieved or angry with yourselves because you sold me here; for God sent me before you to preserve life. ... And God sent me before you to preserve a posterity for you in the earth, and to save your lives by a great deliverance" (Genesis 45:5,7). *To preserve life* in verse 5 means to provide sustenance, revive, quicken, and recover.[8] *Preserve* in verse 7 means to place or set in place, appoint, establish, plant, transform into, and to set or make for a sign.[9] God not only preserved Joseph's life—through Joseph's rising position in Egypt, God went on to preserve the Israelites as well.

"Whoever seeks to save his life will lose it, and whoever loses his life will preserve it" (Luke 17:33). *Preserve* here means "to bring forth alive, to give life, to preserve alive," "to rescue," and "be saved," while in the following verse, *preserve* means "to save, keep safe and sound, to rescue," "deliver or protect," and "make whole."[10,11]

HE IS FAITHFUL

You can see that when you go through pressing times and the good pressing process of the Lord your God, He preserves you. He gives you sustenance. He revives you and gives you quick recovery. Like He did for Joseph, He places you, sets you in place, and appoints you. He establishes you and transforms you. He sets you in to be a sign of His love and goodness to a lost and dying world. He brings you forth alive. He preserves you alive. He rescues you and He saves you. He keeps you safe and sound. He delivers you, protects you, and makes you whole. He does a good work in you!

The Lord your God also uses your life to bless many, even when you do not know it. He allows others to see how you stay close to Him during pressing times. He shows them through your life that He is faithful to preserve you and bring you breakthrough. "Thus says the Lord: 'In an acceptable time I have heard You, and in the day of salvation I have helped You; I will preserve You and give You as a covenant to the people, to restore the earth, to cause them to inherit the desolate heritages'" (Isaiah 49:8). And He shows them that what He does for you, He will do for them too. He uses the pressing times of your life to bring others encouragement and breakthrough as well!

JESUS IS WITH YOU

Stay close to the Lord in the pressures and pressing times of life, and He will preserve you! He has special uses for your life to bless Him and many people, and for you to also be blessed by Him and them.

— Do you believe that the Lord will preserve you in pressing times?

— Do you sometimes feel pressed in between something above and beneath you, like you are stuck in the middle and cannot get out?

God's Zeal for Breakthrough

Jesus is in this pressing process with you. He will never leave you nor forsake you!

— Do you sometimes feel the heavy weight and pressing of life's circumstances?

Jesus is with you, helping you to have breakthrough!

— Do you sometimes feel the heat and pressure of situations pressing in on you?

Jesus comforts you and gives you endurance to press through the pressure!

Notes

[1] "Anointing." Smith's Bible Dictionary. Accessed March 23, 2018. http://www.bible-history.com/smiths/A/Anointing.

[2] "G598 - apothlibō – Strong's Greek Lexicon (NKJV)." Blue Letter Bible. Accessed 13 Mar, 2018. https://www.blueletterbible.org//lang/lexicon/lexicon.cfm?Strongs=G598&t=NKJV.

[3] "G1411 - dynamis – Strong's Greek Lexicon (KJV)." Blue Letter Bible. Accessed 13 Mar, 2018. https://www.blueletterbible.org//lang/lexicon/lexicon.cfm?Strongs=G1411&t=KJV.

[4] "G971 - biazō – Strong's Greek Lexicon (NKJV)." Blue Letter Bible. Accessed 13 Mar, 2018. https://www.blueletterbible.org//lang/lexicon/lexicon.cfm?Strongs=G971&t=NKJV.

[5] Ibid.

[6] "G973 - biastēs - Strong's Greek Lexicon (NKJV)." Blue Letter Bible. Accessed 13 Mar, 2018. https://www.blueletterbible.org//lang/lexicon/lexicon.cfm?Strongs=G973&t=NKJV.

[7] "Preserve." Merriam-Webster.com. Accessed March 23, 2018. https://www.merriam-webster.com/dictionary/preserve.

[8] "H4241 - michyah – Strong's Hebrew Lexicon (NKJV)." Blue Letter Bible. Accessed 13 Mar, 2018. https://www.blueletterbible.org//lang/lexicon/lexicon.cfm?Strongs=H4241&t=NKJV.

[9] "H7760 - suwm – Strong's Hebrew Lexicon (NKJV)." Blue Letter Bible. Accessed 13 Mar, 2018. https://www.blueletterbible.org//lang/lexicon/lexicon.cfm?Strongs=H7760&t=NKJV.

[10] "G2225 - zōogoneō – Strong's Greek Lexicon (NKJV)." Blue Letter Bible. Accessed 13 Mar, 2018. https://www.blueletterbible.org//lang/lexicon/lexicon.cfm?Strongs=G2225&t=NKJV.

[11] "G4982 - sōzō – Strong's Greek Lexicon (NKJV)." Blue Letter Bible. Accessed 13 Mar, 2018. https://www.blueletterbible.org//lang/lexicon/lexicon.cfm?Strongs=G4982&t=NKJV.

— 4 —

God's Authority for Breakthrough

2 SAMUEL 5:20

> *The Lord has broken through my enemies before me, like a breakthrough of water.*

The Lord your God is faithful to give you all that you need. Jesus is the breaker, and He has a breaker anointing to give you breakthrough. "The breaker is come up before them: they have broken up, and have passed through the gate, and are gone out by it: and their king shall pass before them, and the Lord on the head of them" (Micah 2:13 KJV).

THE BREAKER BRINGS THE BREAKTHROUGH

Breaker in the verse above means to break through, break over, break into, break open, break up. It also means to break in pieces, break over limits and increase, burst open, burst out from an enclosure, spread, distribute, break down, break away, grow, and press (through for breakthrough)![1] The Lord is your breaker and does all the above for you. He creates a breakaway for you, hallelujah!

The word *breakthrough* is used only twice in the Bible, and it refers to God breaking through your enemy, like a breakthrough of water:

> So David came to Baal-perazim, and he defeated them there, and said, "The Lord has broken through my enemies before me, like a breakthrough of water." So he named that place Baal-perazim (master of breakthroughs or lord of the breaks).
>
> — 2 Samuel 5:20

> So Israel came up to Baal-perazim, and David defeated the Philistines there. Then David said, "God has broken through my enemies by my hand, like the breakthrough of waters." Therefore they named that place Baal-perazim (master of breakthroughs or lord of the breaks).
>
> — 1 Chronicles 14:11 AMP

Breakthrough here means bursting forth, broken wall, and breaking forth.[2]

THE LORD HAS AUTHORITY TO BRING YOU BREAKTHROUGH

God gives you breakthrough in tough situations to give you victory over the enemy. For example, a bursting forth, a broken wall of water, and a breaking forth of water, like the "waters were a wall" that occurred when God parted the Red Sea. When Pharaoh of Egypt finally let the millions of Israelites leave their enslavement in Egypt, God led them by way of the Red Sea to enter the wilderness. He did this so they could worship Him, the one and only true God, and develop relationship with Him, learn how to enter their promised land, and more. God decided to not allow them to go the short cut into their promised land, but He took them the long way through the wilderness. "Then it came to pass, when Pharaoh had let the people go, that God did not lead them by way of the land of the Philistines, although that was near; for God said, 'Lest perhaps the people change their minds when they see war, and return to Egypt.' So God led the people around by way of the wilderness of the Red Sea" (Exodus 13:17-18).

Before entering the wilderness, God brought the Israelites to the Red Sea. God told Moses to "lift up your rod, and stretch out your hand over the sea and divide it. And the children of Israel shall go on dry ground through the midst of the sea" (Exodus 14:16). One of the meanings of the word *rod* in Hebrew is a scepter. Jesus Christ, the Messiah, is prophesied about as the scepter:

> Your throne, O God, is forever and ever; a scepter of righteousness is the scepter of Your kingdom.
>
> — Psalm 45:6

> I see Him, but not now; I behold Him, but not near; a Star shall come out of Jacob; a Scepter shall rise out of Israel, and batter the brow of Moab, and destroy all the sons of tumult.
>
> — Numbers 24:17

> The scepter shall not depart from Judah, nor a lawgiver from between his feet, until Shiloh comes; and to Him shall be the obedience of the people.
>
> — Genesis 49:10

A scepter is a rod, staff, or baton as a symbol of authority, a mark of authority and ruling.[3] Jesus is this rod, the scepter of righteousness that Moses lifted up in the wilderness. God delivered His people and gave them breakthrough when the enemy pursued them.

> "Then I will harden Pharaoh's heart, so that he will pursue them; and I will gain honor over Pharaoh and over all his

army, that the Egyptians may know that I am the Lord."
. . .

And Moses said to the people, "Do not be afraid. Stand still, and see the salvation of the Lord, which He will accomplish for you today. For the Egyptians whom you see today, you shall see again no more forever. The Lord will fight for you, and you shall hold your peace." And the Lord said to Moses, "Why do you cry to Me? Tell the children of Israel to go forward. But lift up your *rod*, and stretch out your hand over the sea and divide it." . . .

Then Moses stretched out his hand over the sea; and the Lord caused the sea to go back by a strong east wind all that night, and made the sea into dry land, and the waters were divided. So the children of Israel went into the midst of the sea on the dry ground, and the waters were a wall to them on their right hand and on their left."

— Exodus 14:4, 13–16, 21–22; emphasis mine

The Lord then took off the Egyptians' chariot wheels, making the chariots very hard to drive and filling the Egyptians with even more fear of the Lord. Then the Lord told Moses to stretch out his hand over the sea, which he did, and "then the waters returned and covered the chariots, the horsemen, and all the army of Pharaoh that came into the sea after them. Not so much as one of them remained" (v. 28). The Lord gave the Israelites the breakthrough they needed—the bursting forth, the broken walls, and the breaking forth. Dear reader, do not be afraid when the enemy pursues you, but stand still, have faith in the Lord, and trust in Him, and you will see the salvation of the Lord on your behalf!

The Lord uses the pressing battles of your life for many purposes. One is to help you experience victory and breakthrough from Him, and another is for the enemy and people (that the enemy influences) to honor the Lord and to know that He is the Lord. What the Lord did to deliver the Israelites from their enemies, He will do for you!

He will do it!

When you follow the Lord, He will part the waters for you, like a "wall of water" on either side of you to lead you on dry ground to safety. He will break through your enemies like a breakthrough of water! He will deliver you from your enemies and cause them to fear and flee from you because they will see that the Lord fights for you against them and that the Lord God is the Lord! Additionally, the Lord will cause a "wall of water" to come back on your enemies when they flee. The waters will return to their full depth and cover and destroy them, so not one of your enemies remains to harm you! The Lord will save you from "out of the hand" of the enemy! He will give you breakthrough and bring you into the new land that He has for you!

The Lord Jesus goes before you in the pressing battles of your life to take good care of you. He will preserve you. You do not need to take on the battles of life on your own, for the battle is the Lord's. Many times in the Old Testament, when the Israelites came up against the enemy, the Lord required them to not battle the enemy but watch Him, literally, battle for them. Sometimes the Israelites were not called to go to war but called to worship the Lord instead. He went before them as the "breaker" to bring the "breakthrough for them." They just needed to obey Him and do what He told them to do.

> Lift up your heads, O you gates!
> And be lifted up, you everlasting doors!
> And the King of glory shall come in.
> Who is this King of glory?
> The Lord strong and mighty,

> The Lord mighty in battle.
> Lift up your heads, O you gates!
> Lift up, you everlasting doors!
> And the King of glory shall come in.
> Who is this King of glory?
> The Lord of hosts,
> He is the King of glory. *Selah.*
>
> — Psalm 24:7–10

Ask yourself:

- Will I stay close to my Lord Jesus, the King of Glory?
- Will I allow Him to do battle for me and bring me breakthrough?

Notes

[1] "H6555 - parats – Strong's Hebrew Lexicon (NKJV)." Blue Letter Bible. Accessed 13 Mar, 2018. https://www.blueletterbible.org//lang/lexicon/lexicon.cfm?Strongs=H6555&t=NKJV.

[2] "H6556 - perets – Strong's Hebrew Lexicon (NKJV)." Blue Letter Bible. Accessed 13 Mar, 2018. https://www.blueletterbible.org//lang/lexicon/lexicon.cfm?Strongs=H6556&t=NKJV.

[3] "H7626 - shebet – Strong's Hebrew Lexicon (NKJV)." Blue Letter Bible. Accessed 13 Mar, 2018. https://www.blueletterbible.org//lang/lexicon/lexicon.cfm?Strongs=H7626&t=NKJV.

— 5 —

God's Words for Breakthrough

PSALM 62:6; ISAIAH 8:14

> *He only is my rock and my salvation; He is my defense; I shall not be moved. . . . Whoever believes on Him will not be put to shame.*

We frequently go through seasons of life when things don't go the way we want and need them to. We get stuck. We feel that the mountains before us are too high, the circumstances are too difficult, there is no way through. But our Lord God is the God of breakthrough!

WATER IN THE DESERT

The Israelites in the Old Testament felt that they were about to die and there was no hope because they had no water for themselves, their children, or their livestock. In their minds, they were doomed to die and they needed great breakthrough. Their desperation led them to confront and verbally threaten Moses and Aaron. Rather than bring their fear and helplessness to the Lord, they turned it into anger and seemed ready to kill Moses: "And the people complained against Moses, and said, 'Why is it you have brought us up out of Egypt, to kill us and our children and our livestock with thirst?'" (Exodus 17:3). They looked to him as their answer.

But Moses and Aaron knew that God was their only hope and that he was the God of breakthrough. They knew the only way they would get through something that looked like death would be to spend time in His presence and wait on Him to act. They had seen Him do the impossible as they stood before the Red Sea. They were ready to see Him do the impossible again:

> So Moses cried out to the Lord, saying, "What shall I do with this people? They are almost ready to stone me!" And the Lord said to Moses, "Go on before the people, and take with you some of the elders of Israel. Also take in your hand your rod with which you struck the river, and go. Behold, I will stand before you there on the rock in Horeb; and you shall strike the rock, and water will come out of it that the people may drink." And Moses did so in the sight of the elders of Israel.
>
> — Exodus 17:4-6

There were a few million Israelites in the desert, so you can imagine this was a lot of water that came forth. God brought them miracle provision of water from a rock! God split the rock and gave them drink in abundance! God split the rock, and the waters gushed out! Yet again, God made a way where there seemed to be no way.

MOSES DID NOT SPEAK LIFE

The second time the Israelites needed water, they placed their anger on Moses yet again rather than turn to God for breakthrough. They focused not only on the lack of water, but they also brought up the fact that the promises of God couldn't possibly be true because they couldn't see them: "And the people contended with Moses and spoke, saying: 'If only we had died when our brethren died before the Lord! Why have you brought up the assembly of the Lord into this wilderness, that we and our animals should die here? And why have you made us come up out of Egypt, to bring us to this evil place? It is not a place of grain or figs or vines or pomegranates; nor is there any water to drink'" (Numbers 20:3–5).

We do this too—when things are difficult, we sometimes turn to people we think should push through for us. We have fear and focus on what has gone wrong and get angry instead of turning to the God of the breakthrough. Moses and Aaron did what was needed: "Moses and Aaron went from the presence of the assembly to the door of the tabernacle of meeting, and they fell on their faces. And the glory of the Lord appeared to them" (v. 6). When we need breakthrough, we can fall on our faces before God and enter the glory of His presence. In that place, we can see and hear and know far more than we can when we are fearful.

This second time that God wanted to bring forth water of provision from a rock, He told Moses to speak to the rock so that water would come forth to give the Israelites and animals water to drink. But instead of following God's instruction, Moses let his emotions get caught up in the fear and anger of the people around him, and he lost patience. Despite having given up everything he loved to obey the Lord, he knew they blamed him for their predicament, and he let his anger rise up. Rather than let his time with God and God's promise of help restore his peace, "[Moses] said to them, 'Hear now, you rebels! Must we bring water for you out of this rock?'" And rather than follow God's instruction to the letter and speak to the rock, Moses struck the rock twice in anger (vv. 7–11).

Water came from it abundantly, Scripture tells us. All the people and the animals had plenty to drink. Though Moses disobeyed God, God still blessed the Israelites with water. But

Moses had not let God have the glory. He hadn't honored God before the people: "You did not believe Me, to hallow Me in the eyes of the children of Israel" (v. 12). Moses "fixed" the problem his own way by doing what had worked before, while pushing God's better way aside.

God was angry with Moses because striking the rock the first time represented Jesus Christ, the Rock, being struck through his scourging, the crown of thorns that He wore, and His death on the cross. Isaiah 53 is a prophecy about the coming Messiah, Jesus Christ: "Surely He has borne our griefs and carried our sorrows; yet we esteemed Him stricken, smitten by God, and afflicted" (v. 4). Moses was not to strike the rock the second time because Christ, the Rock, was only meant to be struck once and after that He became the spoken Word of life. Moses was supposed to speak life.

God wants to bring you breakthrough, but the best results come about when you spend time in His presence and then follow His every word of direction. If He tells you to do things one way and you default to what worked before, you might miss out on God's best now and in the future. He'll give you the breakthrough, but He wants to be the answer everyone around you sees. He can get the glory when you trust His direction.

God still prevented the deaths of the Israelites, but He took Moses, the man they trusted more than Him, from them—Moses died in the desert. They would enter the promised land without the leader He had chosen for them (Numbers 20:12). They would now be led by God, and more faith would be required to do so.

THE SPIRITUAL ROCK, JESUS CHRIST, GOES WITH YOU

The Israelites drank from the spiritual Rock, Jesus Christ, who led them in the desert:

> Moreover, brethren, I do not want you to be unaware that all our fathers were under the cloud, all passed through the sea, all were baptized into Moses in the cloud and in the sea, all ate the same spiritual food, and all drank the same spiritual drink. For they drank of that spiritual Rock that followed them, and that Rock was Christ.
>
> — 1 Corinthians 10:1–4

Rock in the verses above refers to a mass of rock.[1] Isaiah prophesied about Jesus as "a hiding place from the wind, and a cover from the tempest, as rivers of water in a dry place, as the shadow of a great rock in a weary land" (Isaiah 32:1–3). The Lord Jesus is your rock and salvation. "He only is my rock and my salvation; He is my defense; I shall not be moved" (Psalm 62:6). He can be trusted. He is "a tried stone, a precious cornerstone, a sure foundation" (Isaiah 28:16).

The spiritual Rock, Jesus Christ, followed the Israelites. The word *followed* (in 1 Corinthians 10:4) means He joined as their attendant, accompanied them, was in union with them and on the same road as them.[2] Hallelujah! It's incredible to think that the presence of Christ, the Rock, went with the Israelites in the wilderness to be their living water for forty years![3] Jesus is the living water of life. He provided water to the Israelites in the wilderness. He sustained them with His life. He does the same for you, no matter what you are going through:

> Let him who thirsts come. Whoever desires, let him take the water of life freely.
>
> — Revelation 22:17

> He split the rocks in the wilderness,
> And gave them drink in abundance like the depths.
> He also brought streams out of the rock,
> And caused waters to run down like rivers. . . .

> Behold, He struck the rock,
> So that the waters gushed out,
> And the streams overflowed.
>
> — Psalm 78:15–16, 20

> The Lord lives!
> Blessed be my Rock!
> Let God be exalted,
> The Rock of my salvation!
>
> — 2 Samuel 22:47

Jesus freely gives you the fountain of water of life that springs up into everlasting life!

> Jesus answered and said to her, "Whoever drinks of this water will thirst again, but whoever drinks of the water that I shall give him will never thirst. But the water that I shall give him will become in him a fountain of water springing up into everlasting life."
>
> — John 4:13–14

> If anyone thirsts, let him come to Me and drink. He who believes in Me, as the Scripture has said, out of his heart will flow rivers of living water.
>
> — John 7:37–38

Water and blood from Jesus

Jesus was struck once. When Jesus died on the cross, He pressed through and had breakthrough and gave you breakthrough! "And He, bearing His cross, went out to a place called the Place of a Skull ... where they crucified Him. ... Jesus, knowing that all things were now accomplished, ... said, 'It is finished!' And bowing His head, He gave up His spirit" (John 19:17–18, 28, 30). After Jesus died, "one of the soldiers pierced His side with a spear, and immediately blood and water came out" (John 19:34). This water symbolizes a "breaking forth of water," breakthrough for you.

"For as the heavens are high above the earth, so great is His lovingkindness toward those who fear and worship Him [with awe-filled respect and deepest reverence]" (Psalm 103:11–12 AMP). You can trust Him. When you are going through hard times, spend time in His presence until you feel as if you know what to do. Often, He will give you words to speak over the situation, and He will be with you as you do. Together, you will celebrate as you watch the rock of your hard circumstances split open to give you all the breakthrough you need, and you will be able to walk from a place of death into a new season of life.

God wants to give you breakthrough.

Ask yourself:

— Am I feeling fear, anger, discontentment, and disappointment in my circumstances?

— Will I speak His Words of life to my circumstances?

— Will I seek Him and listen to His instruction that brings me breakthrough?

— Will I trust in His presence and provision for me?

— Will I let His living water give me all I need?

Notes

[1] "G4073 - petra – Strong's Greek Lexicon (NKJV)." Blue Letter Bible. Accessed 23 Mar, 2018.
https://www.blueletterbible.org//lang/lexicon/lexicon.cfm?Strongs=G4073&t=NKJV.

[2] "G190 - akoloutheō – Strong's Greek Lexicon (NKJV)." Blue Letter Bible. Accessed 23 Mar, 2018.
https://www.blueletterbible.org//lang/lexicon/lexicon.cfm?Strongs=G190&t=NKJV.

[3] David Guzik, "Study Guide for 1 Corinthians 10," Blue Letter Bible. Last Modified 21 Feb, 2017.
https://www.blueletterbible.org/Comm/guzik_david/StudyGuide2017-1Cr/1Cr-10.cfm.

II. Your Breakthrough

PRESS through for breakthrough.

P   Pursue God.

R   Rest in God.

E   Emulate Jesus.

S   Sensitize yourself to Holy Spirit.

S   Stand firm in Christ.

— 6 —
Pursue God for Breakthrough

JOHN 10:27

My sheep hear My voice, and I know them, and they follow Me.

P	**Pursue God, your heavenly Father.**
R	Rest in God.
E	Emulate Jesus.
S	Sensitize yourself to Holy Spirit.
S	Stand firm in Christ.

The Lord your God wants a loving relationship with you so you will know and receive His love for you. He also desires you to give your love to Him. He is a gentleman. He won't push Himself upon you or try to make you do something that you do not want to do. He gives you a free will to choose. He hopes that you will choose Him and His ways. "I have chosen the way of truth; Your judgments I have laid before me" (Psalm 119:30). He wants you to pursue Him with all your heart. He wants you to "press" on to know Him and "pursue" the knowledge of Him. The more you know Him and His Word, the more breakthrough you will have.

God wants you to pursue Him because He knows that you need Him and He will always lead you well. He always wants what is best for you. He knows that you can be misguided by the devil—Satan—and earthly wisdom of the world and its ways without His good direction. He knows that you do not have all the answers, but He does. He is the answer:

> Who is wise and understanding among you? Let him show by good conduct that his works are done in the meekness of wisdom. But if you have bitter envy and self-seeking in your hearts, do not boast and lie against the truth. This wisdom does not descend from above, but is earthly, sensual, demonic. For where envy and self-seeking exist, confusion and every evil thing are there.
>
> — James 3:13–16

God wants to help you to walk in His ways. He wants to protect you, preserve you, and grow you into maturity in your walk with Him. He is good and faithful to you. He wants to give you His wisdom. "The wisdom that is from above is first pure, then peaceable, gentle, willing to yield, full of mercy and good fruits, without partiality and without hypocrisy" (James 3:17).

He cares deeply for you. He wants you to hear His voice: "My sheep hear My voice, and I know them, and they follow Me" (John 10:27). He wants to teach you His will in every area of your life so you will flourish, grow, and help people to know Him. "The righteous shall flourish like a palm tree, he shall grow like a cedar in Lebanon. Those who are planted in the house of the Lord shall flourish in the courts of our God" (Psalm 92:12–13). He loves to see how you live for Him.

We must press in to know Him!

Press and pursue Him

The words "let us press" and "pursue" have the same meaning in Hebrew in Hosea 6:3: "Let us acknowledge the Lord. Let us *press* on to know the Lord. As surely as the sun rises, the Lord will appear. He will come to us like the rain, like the spring rain that waters the earth" (HNV, emphasis mine). "Let us know, let us *pursue* the knowledge of the Lord. His going forth is established as the morning; He will come to us like the rain, like the latter and former rain to the earth" (NKJV, emphasis mine).

"Let us press" in the HNV version of Hosea 6:3 means to follow after, run after, chase, attend closely upon, pursue ardently, and aim eagerly to secure. It also means to be pursued.[1] The Lord wants you to follow after Him, run after Him, chase Him, and attend closely upon Him. He also pursues you! He wants you to pursue Him ardently (with warmth of feeling and eagerness, typically expressed in zealous support and activity; fiery and hot, shining and glowing for Him with ardent eyes).[2] He wants you to aim to eagerly secure all that He has for you. "Let us pursue" in the NKJV of Hosea 6:3 means the same as "let us press" does in the HNV translation.[3]

The Lord your God wants you to press on to know Him, to pursue Him, and to follow Him. Everything you need is found in Him. This is why He instructs you to seek Him. He is a loving God who wants to give you what you need.

Pursuit

God pursues you because He loves you deeply. He wants you to pursue Him and receive Him too. When you pursue someone you care about, you are excited and hopeful, and you anticipate being with that person. When you pursue people, you:

- Hope they want fellowship and relationship with you.

- Look expectantly for them, and you are determined to find them.
- Want every opportunity to be with them, even if it's just to look at them or hear their voice.
- Listen to what they say.
- Know being with them will be a longing fulfilled.

A week before my husband, Charles, and I met, God called us independently to go to the same Bible college and the same church. The first night of classes, Charles and I sat down next to each other. After talking with him that night, I knew he would be a good friend. We began talking after classes under the street lights in the parking lot until we saw the college dean lock the building doors. He would give us that smile that said, *It is great that you two are spending time together.* Later, after Charles and I were engaged, the college dean told us that when he first met us independently, the Lord told him that we would be married.

During the beginning of that first semester of Bible college, I was wondering how interested Charles was in me. One day after Sunday church service, almost everyone had left. I was in the foyer, and I saw Charles walk very fast into the foyer and then the bookstore, looking for something or someone, and I felt the Lord say to me, "He is looking for you; he is pursuing you." I was so excited—I felt like I was given a little preview into Charles's heart. I thought, *He likes me; he wants to find me before I leave for the day.* I did not want to miss this opportunity, because I knew if I did not say hi and talk with him, it would be a whole two days before I would see him again in class. That's a very long time when you want to talk with someone you are interested in. I was pursuing Charles too. So I waited for him to come out of the bookstore and we talked for a bit. He told me later that he had, indeed, been looking for me, and I was elated that he was pursuing me and wanted to talk with me. We were both being intentional about our pursuits.

INTENTIONAL PURSUIT

We can be intentional about our pursuit of God: "And whatever you ask in My name, that I will do, that the Father may be glorified in the Son. *If you ask anything in My name, I will do it"* (John 14:13-14, emphasis mine).

FIVE STEPS TO PURSUE GOD:

1. Have faith and believe that God loves you, wants a relationship with you, and has a great plan for your life.
2. Love God and seek His will.
3. Listen to God.
4. Trust God, obey Him, wait on Him, and believe that He will bring you breakthrough.
5. Do God's will at all costs, no matter what the circumstances look or feel like.

1. Have faith and believe that God loves you, wants a relationship with you, and has a great plan for your life.

When you have faith and believe that your Father God, Jesus, and Holy Spirit love you and want a relationship with you, you feel safe and secure with Him. You know that He only wants what is good for you in your life, and you are drawn to Him. You believe that His plans and thoughts for you are good:

> "For I know the plans and thoughts that I have for you," says the Lord, "plans for peace and well-being and not for disaster, to give you a future and a hope. Then you will call on Me and you will come and pray to Me, and I will

hear [your voice] and I will listen to you. Then [with a deep longing] you will seek Me and require Me [as a vital necessity] and [you will] find Me when you search for Me with all your heart. I will be found by you," says the Lord.

— Jeremiah 29:11-14 AMP

You pursue the Lord because you want a relationship with Him too. You are curious about His love for you, and you want to get to know Him more and receive His love and give Him your love. You want to learn from Him and follow Him. "God is love. [He is the originator of love, and it is an enduring attribute of His nature.]" (1 John 4:8 AMP). He likes you, and He loves you, and He wants to bless you!

The Lord your God is a God of relationships. He wants to commune and fellowship with you. You are a part of Him. You are His child, and He loves you. You are a vital part of His family. He never meant for you to live your life on your own. He wants to be your father and mother. He wants to instruct you, teach you how to live, and help you to know the right way to go. He wants to protect you. He wants you to receive Him as your Father God, Jesus as your Lord and Savior, and Holy Spirit as your comforter, teacher, and more. He wants to be your all in all. If your earthly father or mother, or both, were not there to nurture you, I assure you that your heavenly Father God can, and will, heal you of your hurt and loss. He is here for you today and He will be here for you forevermore.

Ask yourself:

- Am I pursuing a close relationship with Father God; Jesus, His Son; and Holy Spirit in my life right now?
- What are some ways I am doing this?
- What are some ways I can do this?

— Have I talked with Him today and told Him about my joys, cares, fears, and more?

2. Love God and seek His will.

Please ask God to help you to love Him more and to show your love for Him. As you spend time with Him, be patient with Him and yourself in letting Him grow that love in you. Love Him, trust Him, and have close fellowship with Him.

Ask God to teach you what His will is and how to do His will. "Teach me to do Your will, for You are my God; Your Spirit is good. Lead me in the land of uprightness" (Psalm 143:10). "And do not be conformed to this world, but be transformed by the renewing of your mind, that you may prove what is that good and acceptable and perfect will of God" (Romans 12:2). As you allow God to transform you by the renewing of your mind, He will help you to know His will. He wants you to renew your mind through meditating on His Word, praising and worshiping Him, and fellowshipping with Him. He also wants you to renew your mind by helping you let go of the things of this world that keep you from Him.

What are some of the trappings of this world that keep you from seeking and knowing His will? They may be intangible things, like having a worldly mind-set of opinions, judgments, and ideas, or things you do and follow that are popular with the world's ways but are opposite to God's ways of truth and life in His Word. They may be relationships or activities that you do and watch that separate you from time with Him, like your TV, computer, or phone. God wants you to have fun in life through your hobbies, individual and group activities, and recreation, but He knows that you need time with Him in His Word to cultivate, maintain, and grow your relationship with Him each day. He misses you and is concerned about you when you do not talk with

Him and include Him in your day's events and decisions. He will show you His will and lead you into breakthrough when you pursue Him in love.

Dear reader, as you read God's Word, you will learn more about Him. You will know Him like you know a person close to you. His Word teaches you who He is, what is important to Him, what pleases Him, and what does not please Him. "For the word of God is living and powerful, and sharper than any two-edged sword, piercing even to the division of soul and spirit, and of joints and marrow, and is a discerner of the thoughts and intents of the heart" (Hebrews 4:12). The more you know God through His Word, the more you will feel His presence with you, and it will be easier for you to know His will for you in all situations in your life. He will give you discernment, understanding, and revelation about your own thoughts, intents, and motivations of your heart (why you do and say the things you do). He will reveal His insight and His will about situations and people as you read His Word. Knowing Him through His Word of truth pleases Him, and He blesses you for doing this. The more you become one with His heart, mind, and will, the greater your breakthrough.

Ask yourself:

- Have I told Him that I love Him today?
- Am I letting Him renew my mind?
- Do I know what God's will is for me in this moment and this season or time of my life?
- What can I do to learn more about God's will for my life today, this week, this month, and this year?

3. Listen to God.

God wants you to hear Him telling you how much He loves you and desires a relationship with you, and about the good things that He wants to do in your life—like fix a challenge in a relationship, develop a ministry, complete a project, help you to overcome problems, or heal you. Ask Him to help you hear what He is saying to you. He loves that you ask Him to help you to know Him, His ways, and His timing more. He wants to help you break through!

Sometimes God will say a lot, and sometimes He will say a little. God loves faith. He wants you to walk by faith and wait on Him until He tells you more. Your faith in Him and your belief in His love for you draws you to Him; it helps you depend on Him. It keeps you in close connection and relationship with Him and helps you to include Him in your life. "Those who are with Him are called, chosen, and faithful" (Revelation 17:14).

Listen to Him, and read His Word each day. He is telling you things and instructing you in all areas of your life throughout the day. He does not want you to miss out on what He is saying to you, because what He says brings you protection, provision, and fulfillment in your life. The more you know God's Word, the more you will know Him and the more you will hear what He says to your heart.

He wants you to hear Him instructing, encouraging, and comforting you. God is love, and He lives in you through the power of His Holy Spirit. You have full access to Him around the clock. He wants you to hear Him because He always leads you on the path of life:

> I will bless the Lord who has given me counsel;
> You will show me the path of life;
> In Your presence is fullness of joy;
> At Your right hand are pleasures forevermore.

> — Psalm 16:7, 11

> For He instructs him in right judgment,
> His God teaches him.
> The Lord of hosts,
> Who is wonderful in counsel and excellent in guidance.
>
> — Isaiah 28:26, 29

He wants to protect you and help you to fulfill all of the wonderful plans that He has for you. When you listen for God's voice and hear His counsel and life-giving words, you will feel safe and secure in Him and yourself. As you listen to Him, your faith will grow and you will expect to see Him bring you the breakthrough that He so wants to give to you.

Ask yourself:

— Do I feel like I can hear Him speaking to my heart?

— Am I asking Him to help me hear Him?

— Am I longing for Him and His comfort and strength?

— Have I told Him that I need Him today?

4. Trust God, obey Him, wait on Him, and believe that He will bring you breakthrough.

When you trust in God, you believe that He loves you and wants the best outcome for you. When you trust Him, you welcome Him in and talk with Him about things that bother you, confuse you, bring you joy, and more! You believe that He has your back, He is watching out for your best interest, and He will bring you breakthrough!

God's way may not always seem easy, but it is the best way. He knows what is best for you, and He wants what is best for you—this is why He leads you in His ways:

> Trust in the Lord with all your heart,

And lean not on your own understanding;
In all your ways acknowledge Him,
And He shall direct your paths.
Do not be wise in your own eyes;
Fear the Lord and depart from evil.
It will be health to your flesh,
And strength to your bones.

— Proverbs 3:5–8

Sadly, when trials, tribulations, and tests come in believers' lives, they sometimes feel that God does not love them or has abandoned them. They lose their trust in Him and run from Him in hurt, anger, and feelings of rejection. But if they are actively reading God's Word of truth and life and are saturated with it, they will surely believe that He loves them. They will choose to keep trusting Him and obeying His Word. They will learn His ways and be able to discern the truth of matters. They'll know when the enemy is trying to detour them from God's good path.

God loves it when you trust in Him and obey His good instruction for you. He wants you to have a heart of obedience toward Him, for this pleases Him. When you do this, you are in essence saying, "God, I trust in you, and I will follow you and do your will, because I love you."

So Samuel said:
"Has the Lord as great delight in burnt offerings and sacrifices,
As in obeying the voice of the Lord?
Behold, to obey is better than sacrifice,
And to heed than the fat of rams."

— 1 Samuel 15:22

If you obey my commands, you will remain in my love,
just as I have obeyed my Father's commands and remain
in his love.

— John 15:10 GNB

You may say, "But you don't know what I've been through and what I've already done! I've loved Him, trusted Him, and obeyed Him, and I'm still waiting for my breakthrough!" Or, "I thought I heard and knew God's will and did it, but things did not work out the way I thought they would." Then keep trusting in Him, obeying, Him, and waiting on Him. He will give you breakthrough because He is good. It may not look the way you want it to or the way you thought it should, but be satisfied with His good answers and ways.

Many times God's answers to your prayers and breakthrough for your needs depend on other people's lives and their readiness and willingness to follow Him. Ask God to help them to pursue Him and follow Him too. Press through as you wait, and keep believing that He will give you breakthrough according to His will and ways. During the waiting process, God is strengthening your faith. Resolve to stand strong in your faith in Him. God is not just interested in the result and what He will do for you and others, but He is very interested in how much you will love Him and seek Him in the process of waiting, pressing, and preparing for the end result. He loves it when you pursue Him and love Him in the waiting-pressing process. This helps you to experience more transformation in your thoughts and feelings, and you become more like Him. The waiting process helps you to handle more anointing, responsibility, and blessings that He gives you at the end of your waiting. He wants you to be closer to Him at the end of the process than you were before the waiting.

Be patient with God, and wait on His timing and confirmations. He is not a drive-through God, where you idle at the window to get a quick answer from Him. He is more like a skilled chef who marinates situations, and you, in the oil of His Holy Spirit. He seasons you in the preparation process (otherwise known as waiting) to make you the best you can be. As is often said, God is never late, He is seldom early, but He is always on time.

Trust is all about relationship with your Father God; Jesus, His Son; and His Holy Spirit. He loves you and knows how good it is for you and those you influence when you are close to Him. There is no end to how close you can get to the Lord your God. His love is so deep and infinite. He wants you to believe in and rest in His love for you. He wants you to experience it as much as you can on earth and to share His love with both those who know Him and those who do not know Him yet—so they will want a deep relationship with Him too: "Then you will know that I am the Lord, for they shall not be ashamed who wait for Me" (Isaiah 49:23).

Ask yourself:

— Can I think of situations now or in the past when I waited for God to bring me breakthrough?

— What are some of the things God is instructing me to do as I wait on Him?

— What is He teaching me in the waiting-pressing process?

— Am I trusting in Him, His goodness, and His love for me as I wait on Him?

— Do I believe He will bring me breakthrough?

5. Do God's will at all costs, no matter what the circumstances look or feel like.

An important reality in God's kingdom is that in life there are challenges. When you are in God's will, the challenges of life do not disappear, but you are cushioned and preserved by His protection, anointing, and provision. "The name of the Lord is a strong tower; the righteous run to it and are safe" (Proverbs 18:10). When you are in the midst of pressing times, you can trust in Him because He knows what He is doing, and He always wants what is best for you. Some challenges are temporary; and some may last for days, months, years, or maybe even a lifetime; but God is faithful to you. He just wants you to surrender your heart to Him and follow Him even when things are not going the way you want them to. He wants you to always have faith in His love for you and in His ability to meet you where you are at in your challenges. When you do this you have, in essence, already received great breakthrough in your way of thinking and understanding. When you surrender your thoughts and beliefs to Him and allow Him to change your perception, you will often gain breakthrough in your circumstances. When you surrender to Him, you allow Him to be Lord of your life; this pleases Him and it opens the way for your breakthrough. He will carry you and give you strength. He also wants you to have faith in His desire and ability to deliver you, heal you, and more! He will give you breakthrough, because you love Him, seek Him, and are willing to do His will at all costs, no matter what the circumstances look or feel like.

I remember when I was sick with a condition for a few years. Halfway through this time, the doctors exhausted their ability to help me, so I told the Lord, "If I have to crawl to serve you, love you, and live for you, I will." I would not give up on His love for me. I believed He knew more about my circumstances and future than I did, and I had peace that He was in charge of my life. I believed that He was doing a good work in me and my family through this challenge. I continued to believe that He would heal me, yet I surrendered this to Him as well. And I chose to believe— if He did not heal me—that He would uphold me, give me strength, and teach me things through this because He is so good and loving. A few years later, I was completely healed. I learned many good things through this challenge, and I became much closer to the Lord through it.

God transforms you by renewing your mind so that you will (prove) know His good and acceptable and perfect will. When God calls you to press through for breakthrough, it's not always easy, and sometimes you need to leave your comfort zone. As you pursue Him, He will help you make wise decisions according to His will and plans for you. He will help you go deeper in relationship with Him, amid your challenges, to develop tenacity, faith, hope, increased love for Him, and so much more.

Be willing to let go of your desires, opinions, thoughts, and even relationships that are not healthy for you; seek to know and do God's will instead. Be willing to learn His ways and do things His way. It is important for you to have a desire to please God rather than to please yourself. Choose to believe that when you do things His way, you will reap a great harvest of blessings in your life. All life flows from Him, and He so wants you to have a fulfilling life. Be willing to recognize that God knows all things and He sees the big picture and every detail. Jesus said, "For whoever does the will of My Father in heaven is My brother and sister and mother" (Matthew 12:50).

But don't be anxious that you may miss His will. He looks at the motivation of your heart first and foremost to see if you want to follow His will. He will cover you and protect you. He will teach you how to hear Him and to know His will. He will teach you to know in your spirit when something is His will and when it is not. His grace will cover you if you miss it, even when you tried to do what is right. He will bring you back on course, for He loves you and is faithful to you!

I often ask God to write His will for me "on the wall" so clearly that I cannot miss it, so I *know that I know* it is His will. Ask Him to give you confirmation through His Word, people, signs, and other ways that He speaks to you, and He will do this. God's timing is perfect, and He is faithful. He is faithful and good! While it is not a law that you need to have two or three confirmations or witnesses attest to what you feel the Lord is leading you to do, He teaches you that this is a good principle in His kingdom: "This will be the third time I am coming to you. 'By the mouth of two or three witnesses every word shall be established'" (2 Corinthians 13:1).

Seek wise counsel and advice from those who are mature in the Lord—people who love Him and have a good track record in hearing Him and doing His will. "One witness shall not rise against a man concerning any iniquity or any sin that he commits; by the mouth of two or three witnesses the matter shall be established" (Deuteronomy 19:15). When you believe that you have confirmation and know God's will, then run with it, and stay focused on doing it at all costs, no matter what the circumstances look or feel like. God will honor and bless your faithfulness and love for Him as you follow Him.

Ask yourself:

— Will I seek God for confirmation on His will?

— Will I do His will when the going gets tough?

— Will I do God's will at all costs, no matter what the circumstances look like or feel like?

— Will I hold on to the Lord with all I've got and press through for breakthrough?

PRAY WITH ME

Father God, thank you for loving me and pursuing me. Please help me to pursue you, Jesus, and Holy Spirit. Fill me with the thrill of anticipation about getting to spend time with you. Tell me what I can do each day to know you more. Guide me to make time to learn who you are in your Word. Please help me to believe you and your Word even more. Help me with any unbelief that I have about your wanting to help me with my problems or other things. Help me to believe strongly in your Word. Help me to believe in your love for me and in the truth of your Word.

God, I'm sorry for not talking with you as much as I can. Guide me to reach out to you more and ask you questions about your thoughts and opinions on things that are going on in my life. Help me to know your will. Help me to follow your instruction. Please help me to hear clearly as you speak to my heart. I don't want to miss hearing you or minimize it because I am so busy. Please bring me confirmations of what you are saying, so I will know it is you speaking to me and not just my own thoughts. Thank you for speaking to me and teaching me your ways.

Father, please help me to love you with all my heart, soul, strength, and mind and to love my neighbor as myself (Luke 10:27). Help me to obey you at all times and to trust you and to stand strong in faith in the waiting seasons. Help me to pursue you, hold on to you with all I've got, and seek to please you as you bring about my breakthrough. In Jesus's name. Amen.

NOTES

[1] "H7291 - radaph – Strong's Hebrew Lexicon (HNV)." Blue Letter Bible. Accessed 14 Apr, 2018.
https://www.blueletterbible.org//lang/lexicon/lexicon.cfm?Strongs=H7291&t=HNV.

[2] "Ardent." Merriam-Webster.com. Accessed April 14, 2018.
https://www.merriam-webster.com/dictionary/ardently.

[3] "H7291 - radaph – Strong's Hebrew Lexicon (NKJV)." Blue Letter Bible. Accessed 14 Apr, 2018.
https://www.blueletterbible.org//lang/lexicon/lexicon.cfm?Strongs=H7291&t=NKJV.

— 7 —

Rest in God

HEBREWS 4:10–11

He who has entered His rest has himself also ceased from his works as God did from His. Let us therefore be diligent to enter that rest.

<u>P</u>	<u>P</u>ursue God, your heavenly Father.
<u>R</u>	**<u>R</u>est in God.**
<u>E</u>	<u>E</u>mulate Jesus.
<u>S</u>	<u>S</u>ensitize yourself to Holy Spirit.
<u>S</u>	<u>S</u>tand firm in Christ.

It is important to rest in God each day. Be still in your heart. Sit with Him. Talk with Him. Train yourself to hear Him. Receive His peace. "Then He arose and rebuked the wind, and said to the sea, 'Peace, be still!' And the wind ceased and there was a great calm" (Mark 4:39). The Lord God teaches you to speak to the storms of life, to trust in Him, and to rest in Him. "Be still, and know that I am God" (Psalm 46:10).

Rest in the Lord your God through:

1. Your activities
2. Faith in Him and trusting Him in pressing times

3. Reading His Word
4. Prayer
5. Praise and worship
6. Receiving inner healing and deliverance
7. Spiritual warfare

1. Your activities

Allow Him to press His goodness and will for you into your life by teaching you a healthy way to live in His rest. Rest in the Lord your God through your activities. Allow Jesus to stretch you and grow you beyond what you know and believe. Be in a restful state of mind as you give your time, energy, finances, and talents in cheerfulness and love. He will use your life to bless others, but He does not want you to strive in the flesh and get worn out. Surrender your ways and schedule to Him. Allow His Holy Spirit to empower you and anoint you in your work and ministry, in your service to your family, friends, and others, and in your rest and recreation. He wants to sustain you with His power and help you to get the most accomplished in the most restful way.

Give your mind, body, emotions, and spirit the deep, rejuvenating sleep that they need each night. Take a power nap when you need to. If you are not sleeping properly, see your doctor and receive prayer and counsel from those who love God. He wants to give you sweet, refreshing sleep that brings healing and strength for each new day.

> Therefore, since a promise remains of entering His rest, let us fear lest any of you seem to have come short of it. ... For we who have believed do enter that rest, ... for He has spoken in a certain place of the seventh day in this way: "And God rested on the seventh day from all His works." ... There remains therefore a rest for the people

of God. For he who has entered His rest has himself also ceased from his works as God did from His. Let us therefore be diligent to enter that rest, lest anyone fall according to the same example of disobedience.

— Hebrews 4:1, 3–4, 9–11

The apostle Paul clearly said to cease from your own works, like working in the flesh and relying on your talents and abilities. There's no rest there. God wants you to follow His ways, and He will give you rest in Him. God rests, and He knows how important and healthy it is for you to rest. God asks mankind to have a Sabbath day of rest. He wants the promise of rest for your mind, emotions, body, and spirit. Rest, contentment, joy, and peace come from following Him and walking closely with Him. As you rest in the Lord, rely on Him, trust in Him, and abide in Him—the Vine—you will develop healthy fruit of the Spirit in your life.

Allow His peace to guard your heart and mind. He wants you to be in a state of rest in all that you do. He wants you to be flexible, like a rubber band that stretches with ease. He wants you to look at your life to see if your thinking, emotions, and behaviors are led by Him. If they are not, then ask Him how to make good changes, for He has given you the mind of Christ: "For 'who has known the mind of the Lord that he may instruct Him?' But we have the mind of Christ" (1 Corinthians 2:16). It takes practice, but you can do it. Choose to meditate on "whatever things are true, whatever things are noble, whatever things are just, whatever things are pure, whatever things are lovely, whatever things are of good report. . . . The things which you learned and received and heard and saw in me, these do, and the God of peace will be with you" (Philippians 4:8–9). Ask the Lord what He wants you to learn from the situations you are in and allow Him to instruct you. He will give you revelation, understanding, and peace and help you to rest in Him.

Rest in God

At one point in the ministry years ago, I was doing, doing, doing, and I got burnt out. I asked the Lord, "Why do I feel numb and frozen over?" He answered in a loving way, "You have been eating from the Tree of Knowledge of Good and Evil." I knew immediately in my spirit what the Lord meant, even though I had never heard this term used for a challenge I had been in before. I had not been eating from the Tree of Life. I had not been spending time in His presence or walking in the Spirit nor relying on Him more and less on myself, my thoughts, and my own abilities. "The Lord God planted a garden eastward in Eden, and there He put the man whom He had formed. And out of the ground the Lord God made every tree grow that is pleasant to the sight and good for food. The tree of life was also in the midst of the garden, and the tree of the knowledge of good and evil" (Genesis 2:8–9).

The Lord your God wants you to have rest by including Him and welcoming Him in what you do. His Holy Spirit lives in you, and He wants you to acknowledge His presence. He wants you to have fun with Him in your activities.

One day I heard the Lord say to my heart, "I ordained rest. I want it for you, and it is a good thing!" This gave me relief deep in my spirit knowing that God created man to rest, not just on the Sabbath but in man's doing throughout the week. I studied this in the Word, and I received its truth, and I felt no shame or guilt about not working so hard. I began taking my time in doing things and resting in Him. I realized I had missed out for many years of rest, but now God was teaching me the correct way to live.

Then after this, Father God said to me, "You have a right to be here on the earth." Wow! I had gone through inner healing and deliverance and had grown a lot in the Lord over the years, but when He said this, it touched me to my core and brought deep healing and understanding in three seconds! I did not know that I had not felt worthy or wanted here on earth, but when I looked deep inside my heart and mind, I saw that the effects of neglect and abuse from my childhood had taken their toll. I still believed some lies from the enemy about my worth—of which I was not even conscious. These lies were not just in my mind but deep seated in my emotions and my spirit. They had become part of my way of living. I began to truly accept God's love for me and to rest in Him and His love in a new and deeper way. I found the more I absorbed God's Word in my thoughts, the more my emotions were transformed, and I had more joy and hope.

God truly loves you as you are. He takes you as you are and molds and shapes you into a vessel that can hold more anointing and responsibility. He can help you to give more of Him to others. You can be restful as you participate in any hobby—physical exercise; viewing beauty in nature, arts, and crafts; writing poetry; singing—and so many other things that heighten your awareness of the Spirit of God in and around you. Rest by having hobbies that bring you joy, contentment, and peace of heart. Allow God's Holy Spirit to lead your body, mind, emotions, and spirit into joy, freedom, hope, and peace.

In another instance a few years ago, I was working hard and I hit the wall, so to speak—physically, mentally, emotionally, and spiritually—and I needed to rest. Through this time of healing and resting in God, I came to see that I had been driven by some anxiety that had become a way of life for me since childhood. I was finding my value in doing what I felt was necessary rather than seeing my value in who the Lord said I was. I needed to only do what He wanted me to do and to rest in Him while doing it. He wanted me to rest with Him. He knows how to rest very well.

I needed to learn how to rest in my activities throughout the day by communing with Him and being directed by Him. I also needed to learn how to pace myself with downtime in between activities. I started to allow the Lord to lead me, and I found that my mind, emotions, body, and spirit entered into more healing and rest the more I rested in Him. He led me in simple ways like taking deep breaths and releasing them slowly, stretching my muscles, walking, talking with Him and telling Him what I think and feel, asking Him questions and listening to His response and instructions, praising Him, and thanking Him and telling Him how much I need Him and love Him. God is faithful to give you wisdom and solutions in your everyday situations in your work, relationships, ministry, and more.

Try to not be too busy, doing and working, even in ministry for God. Bring a healthy balance of work, play, and rest into your life. It is important to pace yourself to be healthy and at ease. God will take your relationship with Him to a new level when you talk with Him, commune with Him, and include Him in what you do. He loves to commune with you and give you revelation, wisdom, and protection at all times, not just in your times of pressing. He created you to enjoy your life and to do things that bring you joy and rest in your mind, emotions, body, and spirit.

Ask the Lord:

- What do you want my schedule to look like today, tomorrow, and the rest of this week?
- When do you want me to take a break during the day?
- How do you want me to rest during and between activities?
- Please help me to include you in my activities and decisions by talking with you, listening to you, and following you each day.

2. Faith in Him and trusting Him in pressing times

Rest in the Lord your God through faith in Him. When you release to the Lord any fears, worries, burdens, and unbelief of His willingness and ability to take good care of you, you are choosing to rest in Him. The Lord blesses you as you hold on to Him and rest in Him each time you take a step of faith. As you grow in trusting Him, He will help you to take big leaps of faith instead of steps. Faith is like glue—it keeps you holding on to Him with everything you've got. When you exercise your faith, the Lord uses it to take you on adventures with Him. He rewards your faith. You enter into the supernatural, unseen realm through your faith. You connect with Him and can rest in knowing that He is always good and He only wants good things for you. He is faithful to you, and He loves your faith in Him. "Now faith is the substance of things hoped for, the evidence of things not seen. . . . But without faith it is impossible to please Him, for he who comes to God must believe that He is, and that He is a rewarder of those who diligently seek Him" (Hebrews 11:1, 6). [Hebrews 11 is known as "The Hall of Faith." It is full of power and joy, as it heralds those in the Old Testament who lived by faith. It is a wonderful demonstration and inspiration on how you, too, can live by faith! Please see Appendix B for the outline of the entire chapter of Hebrews 11, "The Hall of Faith."]

Rest in the Lord your God through trusting Him in pressing times. Jesus gives you peace in Him and joy in tribulation knowing that He has overcome the world! "These things I have spoken to you, that in Me you may have peace. In the world you will have tribulation; but be of good cheer, I have overcome the world" (John 16:33). He gives you hope and encouragement to hang in there and to never, ever give up, because "in due season we shall reap if we do not lose heart" (Galatians 6:9).

You can always run to Him because you trust He is your refuge. You abide in Him and He gives you His peace. Jesus calls out to you, "Come to Me, all you who labor and are heavy laden, and I will give you rest. Take My yoke upon you and learn from Me, for I am gentle and lowly in heart, and you will find rest for your souls. For My yoke is easy and My burden is light" (Matthew 11:28–30). Give Him every burden, and rest in Him. He wants you to learn from Him in the pressing times. He knows what is best for you, and He always wants the best for you!

Ask the Lord:

— Search my heart and show me any fears, worries, burdens, and unbelief I may have that I can release to you.

— What steps of faith would you like me to take this week?

— What can I learn from you in these pressing times?

3. Reading His Word

Rest in the Lord your God through reading His Word. Reading, meditating on, and absorbing God's Word is vital to your entering His rest. God's Word is truth, and when you read it, digest it, and live it, it will help you to discern the truth and intentions of your heart and of your soul (mind, will, and emotions). Is what you choose to do life-giving in the Spirit? The Word will let you know and will help you to make wise decisions.

When you are not reading His Word—seeking God on how to do things His way—you are not trusting in nor obeying Him. This form of independence can keep you from having the peace He wants for you. God wants you to keep His living Word alive in your heart—as your compass on how to walk with Him. He wants you to read His Word and process it in your body as a powerful, living food, full of nutrients, to keep you strong and healthy. He wants you to include Him in your days and nights by talking with Him and listening to Him speak through His Word. Do not rely on your own strength that is limited. His Word will preserve you and give you His strength so you will have breakthrough.

Ask the Lord:

— Lord, who do you say that I am in your Word of Life?
— Is there anything I have chosen to do that is not life-giving in the Spirit?
— Please show me every life-giving choice I can make in your Word that will help me press through.

4. Prayer

Rest in the Lord your God through prayer. God wants you to pray to Him and talk with Him, Jesus, and Holy Spirit about your thoughts, needs, and the needs of others. He wants you to tell Him how much you love Him and to share your feelings and your pain with Him. He wants you to ask Him questions on what to do, to ask for forgiveness, to forgive others, and then to listen to what He says to your heart. Also, learn how God initiates conversations with you, how He talks with you, and how He responds to your thoughts, feelings, and questions to Him.

Consider having time each day where you journal what you hear God speaking to your heart. Talk with Him throughout the day, commune with Him, abide in Him. Ask Him to help you to do this, and He will. It will bring you peace, rest, and security in Him. Stay close to Him so you will hear His direction on what to do and not do. Be patient and wait for Him. Be attentive to Him. He may answer your questions when you ask Him, or He may add to His response throughout the day, or He may respond for the first time at a later time. Allow Him to lead you so you will make wise decisions in big and small ways. He wants to protect you and

Rest in God

give you breakthrough. He is always faithful to guide you in His truth.

Jesus teaches you how to pray in what is known as the Lord's Prayer, below:

> Your Father knows the things you have need of before you ask Him. In this manner, therefore, pray:

> Our Father in heaven,
> Hallowed be Your name.
> Your kingdom come.
> Your will be done
> On earth as it is in heaven.
> Give us this day our daily bread.
> And forgive us our debts,
> As we forgive our debtors.
> And do not lead us into temptation,
> But deliver us from the evil one.
> For Yours is the kingdom and the power and the glory forever. Amen.

> For if you forgive men their trespasses, your heavenly Father will also forgive you. But if you do not forgive men their trespasses, neither will your Father forgive your trespasses.
>
> — Matthew 6:5-15

Jesus teaches you how to pray to your heavenly Father and about what is important to Him. You are not limited to pray to Father God only, for He gives you freedom to pray to Him, Jesus, and Holy Spirit, as they are one. I talk with each and pray to each as I feel led at different times.

Father God gives you great grace. I do not exclude Him, and I don't feel that He is offended, if I address Jesus or Holy Spirit at a particular moment, for He knows that I love Him and I'm just feeling the need to talk and pray to one of them. "And whatever you ask in My name, that I will do, that the Father may be glorified in the Son. If you ask anything in My name, I will do it" (John 14:13–14). Your Father God loves you deeply, and He gives you great grace. Father, Jesus, and Holy Spirit are very happy that you talk with them, pray to them, ask for their advice, and tell them how much you love them and need them. "In everything by prayer and supplication, with thanksgiving, let your requests be made known to God; and the peace of God, which surpasses all understanding, will guard your hearts and minds through Christ Jesus" (Philippians 4:6–7). As you pray and ask God to supply your needs and you thank Him, He gives you deep peace. Anticipate with joy that He will answer you and guide you well. [Please see Appendix C regarding praying to Father God, Jesus, and Holy Spirit. Please see Appendix D for definitions and Scripture references on the differences between prayer, supplication, petition, and intercession.]

Ask the Lord:

— Please teach me how you initiate conversations with me, how you talk with me, and how you respond to my thoughts, feelings, and questions to you.

— Please teach me how to commune and abide with you throughout the day.

— Please teach me how to give thanks always.

5. Praise and worship

Rest in the Lord your God through praise and worship. Your body, mind, emotions, and spirit enter into deep rest, joy, and renewal when you praise and worship God. Worship with quiet or jubilant music, singing, and shouts of joy. "Oh come, let us sing to the Lord! Let us shout joyfully to the Rock of our salvation" (Psalm

95:1). Wave banners and flags and more by yourself or with a congregation of people:

> Praise the Lord!
>
> Praise God in His sanctuary;
> Praise Him in His mighty firmament!
>
> Praise Him for His mighty acts;
> Praise Him according to His excellent greatness!
>
> Praise Him with the sound of the trumpet;
> Praise Him with the lute and harp!
>
> Praise Him with the timbrel and dance;
> Praise Him with stringed instruments and flutes!
>
> Praise Him with loud cymbals;
> Praise Him with clashing cymbals!
> Let everything that has breath praise the Lord.
>
> Praise the Lord!"
>
> — Psalm 150

During praise and worship to God, you are releasing your cares to Him, thanking Him, celebrating Him, honoring Him, and glorifying Him and His Name. "I will worship toward Your holy temple, and praise Your name for Your lovingkindness and Your truth; for You have magnified Your word above all Your name" (Psalm 138:2). You come into great unity with Him, Jesus, and Holy Spirit when you praise and worship Him. You are singing words of life that create and bring new life and rejuvenation to the people and atmosphere around you. Praise gives you hope!

When you enter into praise and worship, especially when you do not feel like it or are too busy or other things deter you, your praise and worship is a sweet sacrifice to the Lord. He honors you for doing it. "By Him let us continually offer the sacrifice of praise to God, that is, the fruit of our lips, giving thanks to His name" (Hebrews 13:15).

Praise and worship to God gives you freedom from the weights and heaviness of the cares of this world. God gives you breakthrough during praise and worship! He speaks to your heart, and He revives your mind, body, emotions, and spirit. He sees that you are trusting in Him and loving Him, and this pleases Him.

Praise and worship is another way to diligently seek God. You exercise your faith during praise and worship. God's angels move on your behalf, and God accomplishes a lot—for you are focusing on Him and not yourself or your problems. You are surrendering to Him, and He loves this. Praise and worship brings you into a closer relationship with Him. He gives you rest, strength, joy, peace, solutions to your needs, and so much more.

Ask the Lord:

— Please help me to enter into praise and worship no matter how I feel or how busy I am.

— Show me the breakthrough you give during praise and worship.

— Thank you for the freedom you bring through worship.

6. Receiving inner healing and deliverance

Rest in the Lord your God through receiving inner healing and deliverance from oppression. There are times when you may need inner healing, deliverance, and counseling from the hurts of life and oppression of the enemy. God uses this to give rest to your mind, heart, body, and spirit. Past hurts, oppression, sins, and generational family patterns that you have learned can negatively affect your thoughts and behaviors. Ask God to reveal any hurts, stressors, anxiety, and fears in your life. Ask Him to give you courage to face them and to overcome. He is faithful to do this, and He will face them with you.

God wants to heal you and give you rest in your soul (mind, will, and emotions).

> He who dwells in the secret place of the Most High
> Shall abide under the shadow of the Almighty.
> I will say of the Lord, "He is my refuge and my fortress;
> My God, in Him I will trust."
>
> Surely He shall deliver you from the snare of the fowler
> And from the perilous pestilence.
> He shall cover you with His feathers,
> And under His wings you shall take refuge.
>
> — Psalm 91:1–4

He will deliver you from the snares of the enemy. He will protect you, heal you, and surround you with songs of deliverance. "You are my hiding place; You shall preserve me from trouble; You shall surround me with songs of deliverance. *Selah*" (Psalm 32:7). He will hide you and preserve you from trouble. "Because he has set his love upon Me, therefore I will deliver him; I will set him on high, because he has known My name. He shall call upon Me, and I will answer him; I will be with him in trouble; I will deliver him and honor him. With long life I will satisfy him, and show him My salvation" (Psalm 91:14–16).

He will take you out of the hot scorching sun of the hurts of life, tuck you away in the cleft of the rock, and minister sweet rest and refreshing to you. "So it shall be, while My glory passes by, that I will put you in the cleft of the rock, and will cover you with My hand while I pass by" (Exodus 33:22). He will give you a new way of living in Him full of freedom, joy, and breakthrough! "O my dove, in the clefts of the rock, in the secret places of the cliff, let me see your face, let me hear your voice; for your voice is sweet, and your face is lovely" (Song of Solomon 2:14).

Ask the Lord:

— Are there any hurts, stressors, anxiety, or fears in my life you wish to heal?
— Thank you for the courage to face them and to overcome.
— Help me to trust that you will protect me, heal me. and surround me with songs of deliverance.

7. Spiritual warfare

The Lord your God wants you to rest in Him when you feel spiritual warfare from the enemy. Sometimes the best thing you can do is take a nap when the enemy's arrows fly toward you. Yes, you keep your armor on, but sometimes the Lord does not want you to go to war. Back in the early '90s, I would fight the enemy head on through a lot of prayer, praise, and worship. I'd read and declare the Word of God and more. These are all good, but I would focus too much on the enemy and my fears, exert myself more than I needed to, and then get exhausted. I did not seek the Lord on how and when to do spiritual warfare; I just went for it when I felt the enemy's attacks.

Years later, God taught me that He ordained rest. I learned His strategies in His Word on what to do in spiritual warfare, and I changed my efforts. I began to seek Him on how and when He wanted me to engage in spiritual warfare, and instead of fighting the enemy, I learned how to outsmart him. I discovered that he is not smart after all, and that God's strategies always cause us to win!

> Abide in Me, and I in you. As the branch cannot bear fruit of itself, unless it abides in the vine, neither can you, unless you abide in Me. . . . If you abide in Me, and My words abide in you, you will ask what you desire, and it shall be done for you. By this My Father is glorified, that you bear much fruit; . . . and that your fruit should remain, that whatever you ask the Father in My name He may give you.
>
> — John 15:4, 7–8, 16

Dear reader, I encourage you be diligent in your faith and in God's will when you are in spiritual warfare. Some days you may feel spiritual warfare in the atmosphere around you or in certain locations or territories. Some days you may feel it when you are at home, when you drive in traffic, or when you are at work. It may be warfare directed at you personally, or you may be feeling warfare that is happening in your city or nation. It is important for you to ask the Lord if He wants you to engage in battle, when to do it, and how much to praise and worship Him or declare His Word. "'Not by might nor by power, but by My Spirit,' says the Lord of hosts" (Zechariah 4:6).

The Lord told King Jehoshaphat and the Israelites to watch Him do battle for them, and He delivered them without their ever having to go into battle (2 Chronicles 20). He can do the same for you. There are times when the Lord wants you to actively participate in battle warfare against the enemy with the authority the Lord has given you in order to nullify the enemy's efforts, but God always wants you to stay connected to Him and follow His instructions. He wants you to be strong and wise during spiritual warfare. He wants to protect you, preserve you, and give you breakthrough.

You may also feel spiritual warfare directed at you through people not following the Lord or people who do know the Lord but are operating in their human fleshly nature. They are allowing the enemy to influence them to falsely accuse, condemn, judge, and hurt you or to hurt your relationship with them or with others. When this happens, it is also important to seek the Lord regarding if and how He wants you to engage in battle with the enemy affecting these people's lives and relationships. Spiritual warfare for people—especially for those you are in close relationships with (personal, business, ministerial, or other)—can take a lot of time, energy, and persistence before you see breakthrough. In these cases you will be in much prayer, seeking the Lord and engaging in His strategies to help these people break free from the enemy's grip and to preserve your relationship with them.

Then there are no guarantees that they will choose to learn from the Lord what they need as you love them and stand in the gap for them. At the end of the day, they will make the choice to see and receive God's truth or not, to see how the enemy lies to them and seeks to steal, kill, and destroy them and their relationships. When the Lord asks you to engage in battle for people, He wants you to use His strategies to expose the works of the enemy in their lives. Additionally, He wants you to usher in the Holy Spirit in their lives to help them to receive Him, His love, and His wisdom for them.

Sometimes when you do spiritual warfare on behalf of people and your relationship with them, God may have you not talk with them about it at first, or ever. They may not be able to deal with the truth of their partnering with the enemy against you. So sometimes you must do it silently through your prayers and your behavior of displaying God's love and truth to them in a way that they can receive it.

It is important for you to know what God's will is and that you are in His will because tests, trials, tribulations, temptations, and spiritual warfare will come. When you know that God called you into a certain situation or relationship, you will persevere, hang in there, and not quit, for you know that He will bring breakthrough!

Ask the Lord:

- When I have challenges at work with my assignments or people, what do you want me to do and not do to be at rest in you and with you?
- Do you want me to help them see areas of their lives you are exposing so they can change and grow?
- Do you want to preserve my relationship with them?
- How can I help them see the enemy is lying to them about me? Should I wait on you, respond to them, talk with them, not talk with them, pray, worship, or is there something else you would like me to do?
- What do you want to teach them, and me, through my standing in the gap for them?

PRAY WITH ME

Lord, please help me to not carry burdens but to cast my cares upon you and rest in you. Please show me how to do this with my thoughts, actions, and emotions.

Help me to find my value in you and to rest in you. Help me to seek you on what you want me to do each day and how you want me to do it. Guide me to quickly recognize when stressors begin to negatively affect me physically, emotionally, mentally, and spiritually. Help me to stop the cycle of reacting to them in negative ways that cause me anxiety and heartache.

Guide me to rest in you, even in the busiest of days. Help me to react to stressors in a positive, restful way that brings me life and steadiness. Guide me to talk with you and receive your love and thoughts throughout the day. Help me to include you in my activities and to hear all that you are teaching me and sharing with me. Lord, thank you that you support me and cheer me on so I can overcome and have breakthrough!

— 8 —
Emulate Jesus for Breakthrough

MARK 3:14

He appointed twelve, that they might be with Him and that He might send them out.

P	**P**ursue God, your heavenly Father.
R	**R**est in God.
E	**Emulate Jesus.**
S	**S**ensitize yourself to Holy Spirit.
S	**S**tand firm in Christ.

Jesus asks you to emulate Him—to imitate Him or try to be like Him.[1] You can do this by doing what He taught you to do in the Gospels and by what the apostle Paul taught through the Holy Spirit in the New Testament's Epistles. Jesus wants you to be like Him. He wants you to show people His heart of love and how to live as a Christian—a disciple of Christ.

Disciples

Jesus's dad, Joseph, and his mom, Mary, lived in the town of Nazareth in the Galilean region. Jesus was born in Bethlehem, but He grew up in Nazareth. He was a Galilean and was trained as a rabbi in Galilee. After Jesus was tempted in the wilderness by Satan, He began his ministry in Galilee. "From that time Jesus began to preach and to say, 'Repent, for the kingdom of heaven is at hand'" (Matthew 4:17).

The most famous rabbis came from Galilee at the time of Jesus. They loved the Scriptures and were passionately faithful to them. A Galilean rabbi was very particular about who he chose as his *talmidim*—disciples. He taught them Scriptures and how to apply them to their lives. The disciples were totally committed to their rabbi, and they had a very close relationship with him, and he with them. The disciples spent all of their time with their rabbi—listening, observing, learning, and imitating by doing what he taught them so they could be like him. They followed their rabbi without knowing where he would lead them, but they trusted him. Eventually, the disciples would become teachers too.

It was a great honor to the twelve disciples that Jesus, their rabbi, asked them to follow Him and be His disciples or talmidim:

> And Jesus, walking by the Sea of Galilee, saw two brothers, Simon called Peter, and Andrew his brother, casting a net into the sea; for they were fishermen.
>
> Then He said to them, "Follow Me, and I will make you fishers of men." They immediately left their nets and followed Him.
>
> Going on from there, He saw two other brothers, James the son of Zebedee, and John his brother, in the boat with Zebedee their father, mending their nets. He

called them, and immediately they left the boat and their father, and followed Him.

— Matthew 4:18–22

He went up on the mountain and called to Him those He Himself wanted. And they came to Him. Then He appointed twelve, that they might be with Him and that He might send them out.

— Mark 3:13–14

Since Jesus chose them, they knew that He believed they had the ability to learn from Him and become like Him. This affirmed them and gave them hope and confidence to believe in themselves, especially when it was difficult for them to follow Him. Jesus told them, "A disciple is not above his teacher, but everyone who is perfectly trained will be like his teacher" (Luke 6:40). They emulated Jesus.

The Lord Jesus wants you to be His talmidim, His disciple. He wants you to imitate Him and be like Him. He wants this to be a priority in your life. He wants you to be passionate about your love for Him and your love for learning and living His Word of life and truth. He wants to have a very close relationship with you and for you to desire the same. He wants you to follow Him and trust Him, even when you do not know where He is leading you.

As you grow in your walk with the Lord Jesus, He wants you to teach, demonstrate, and be a light to those who do not know Him yet and to believers as well. Jesus wants you to train them to imitate Him and become like Him too. You do not need to be an official teacher or have a degree to teach and train others how to love and follow Jesus; you just live your life as an example, and they will see Him in you and learn from you. Jesus empowers you by His Holy Spirit to emulate Him, and this gives you breakthrough!

Love

When you imitate Jesus, you truly reflect what Jesus said are the two greatest commandments—to love God and your neighbor:

> One of the scribes came, and having heard them reasoning together, perceiving that He had answered them well, asked Him, "Which is the first commandment of all?" Jesus answered him, "The first of all the commandments is: 'Hear, O Israel, the Lord our God, the Lord is one. And you shall love the Lord your God with all your heart, with all your soul, with all your mind, and with all your strength.' This is the first commandment. And the second, like it, is this: 'You shall love your neighbor as yourself.' There is no other commandment greater than these."
>
> — Mark 12:28–31

If you do these two greatest commandments—love God and love your neighbor—and demonstrate this in your life, then you are more likely to succeed in following God's Ten Commandments. The Hebrew word for *neighbor* in Exodus 20:17 can also mean "friend, another, fellow, companion, brother, husband, or lover."[2] [When we seek to emulate Jesus, we need to remember that there are things only He can do. Please see Appendix E for more examples.]

The main markers we can learn from when it comes to emulating Jesus are the following:

1. Completely surrender to and obey Him.
2. Be filled and led by the Holy Spirit.
3. Praise and worship God and pray to Him.
4. Love like Jesus—be compassionate, kind, and filled with grace.

5. Be filled with the Word.
6. Be humble and a servant to all.
7. Lead others and fulfill the Great Commission.

1. Completely surrender to and obey Him.

Jesus was heard because of His submission to the Father. "During the days of Jesus' life on earth, he offered up prayers and petitions with fervent cries and tears to the one who could save him from death, and he was heard because of his reverent submission. Son though he was, he learned obedience from what he suffered" (Hebrews 5:7–8 NIV). We are to "submit to God. Resist the devil and he will flee from you" (James 4:7), which Jesus modeled for us.

We stay in His love by obeying His commands, just like Jesus did. "If you keep My commandments and obey My teaching, you will remain in My love, just as I have kept My Father's commandments and remain in His love" (John 15:10 AMP). Our desire needs to be to obey Him and to refuse to entertain any sinful thoughts that would pull us away from that obedience:

> If anyone desires to come after Me, let him deny himself, and take up his cross daily, and follow Me.
> — Luke 9:23

> Our old man was crucified with Him, that the body of sin might be done away with, that we should no longer be slaves of sin. For he who has died has been freed from sin. Now if we died with Christ, we believe that we shall also live with Him, knowing that Christ, having been raised from the dead, dies no more. Death no longer has dominion over Him. For the death that He died, He died to sin once for all; but the life that He lives, He lives to

God. Likewise you also, reckon yourselves to be dead indeed to sin, but alive to God in Christ Jesus our Lord.

— Romans 6:6-11

The apostle Paul said, "But put on the Lord Jesus Christ, and make no provision for the flesh, to gratify its desires" (Romans 13:14), with the solution being to "walk in the Spirit, and you shall not fulfill the lust of the flesh" (Galatians 5:6). If Jesus was holy, we can emulate Him and be holy too.

2. Be filled and led by the Holy Spirit.

Jesus was filled with the Holy Spirit when He was baptized by John the Baptist, and after that He "returned from the Jordan and was led by the Spirit into the wilderness" (Luke 4:1). We are filled with Holy Spirit when we ask Him to come and fill us, just like the disciples in the time of Acts. "And when they had prayed, the place where they were assembled together was shaken; and they were all filled with the Holy Spirit" (Acts 4:31). We're considered sons of God when we let His Holy Spirit lead us, "for as many as are led by the Spirit of God, these are sons of God" (Romans 8:14).

When we are filled with Jesus, we can have His mind and think like Him, making it easy to be led by Him:

Do not conform to the pattern of this world, but be transformed by the renewing of your mind.

Then you will be able to test and approve what God's will is—his good, pleasing and perfect will.

— Romans 12:1-2 NIV

Whatever things are true, whatever things are noble, whatever things are just, whatever things are pure, whatever things are lovely, whatever things are of good report, if there is any virtue and if there is anything praiseworthy—meditate on these things. The things which you learned and received and heard and saw in me, these do, and the God of peace will be with you.

— Philippians 4:8–9

3. Praise and worship God and pray to Him.

Jesus was always ready to praise His Father and thank Him. "At that time Jesus, full of joy through the Holy Spirit, said, 'I praise you, Father, Lord of heaven and earth, because you have hidden these things from the wise and learned, and revealed them to little children. Yes, Father, for this is what you were pleased to do'" (Luke 10:21 NIV). We are to do the same. "Therefore by Him let us continually offer the sacrifice of praise to God, that is, the fruit of our lips, giving thanks to His name" (Hebrews 13:15).

The chief way to worship God in a way that pleases Him is to worship from our spirit and with the truth of the Word. "The hour is coming, and now is, when the true worshipers will worship the Father in spirit and truth; for the Father is seeking such to worship Him. God is Spirit, and those who worship Him must worship in spirit and truth" (John 4:23–24).

Jesus loved to communicate to His Father through prayer because He recognized His need for a very close relationship with Father God. He wants us to do the same. "Now in the morning, having risen a long while before daylight, He went out and departed to a solitary place; and there He prayed" (Mark 1:35). "So He Himself often withdrew into the wilderness and prayed" (Luke 5:16).

> ### 4. Love like Jesus—be kind, compassionate, forgiving, and merciful.

Love is God's highest value, and when we love one another, we emulate Jesus the most. "Above all things have fervent love for one another, for 'love will cover a multitude of sins.'" (1 Peter 4:8). God wants us to love and give without grumbling, because a bad attitude can tarnish love. "Be hospitable to one another without grumbling . . . that in all things God may be glorified through Jesus Christ, to whom belong the glory and the dominion forever and ever. Amen" (1 Peter 4:9, 11). We are to "walk in the way of love, just as Christ loved us and gave himself up for us as a fragrant offering and sacrifice to God" (Ephesians 5:2 NIV).

Walking in love looks like living like Jesus. He was kind and thoughtful and never looked for revenge. On the contrary, He looked for ways to bless people and let them know they were loved. He knew that to be a blessing meant He would walk in blessing. "Finally, all of you be of one mind, having compassion for one another; love as brothers, be tenderhearted, be courteous; not returning evil for evil or reviling for reviling, but on the contrary blessing, knowing that you were called to this, that you may inherit a blessing" (1 Peter 3:8–9). Jesus always saw and understood what people were going through, and He made sure they felt cared for and loved. "But when He saw the multitudes, He was moved with compassion for them, because they were weary and scattered, like sheep having no shepherd" (Matthew 9:36).

Jesus was also always ready to forgive, because He understood the reason why people did the things they did, and that many times it was because they lacked understanding: "Then Jesus said, 'Father, forgive them, for they do not know what they do'" (Luke 23:34). He emphasized how important it was for us to do the same. "Be kind and compassionate to one another, forgiving each other, just as in Christ God forgave you" (Ephesians 4:32 NIV).

Jesus taught us that when we are filled with God's love, we can be merciful and give and keep on giving:

> But I say to you who hear: Love your enemies, do good to those who hate you, bless those who curse you, and pray for those who spitefully use you. To him who strikes you on the one cheek, offer the other also. And from him who takes away your cloak, do not withhold your tunic either. Give to everyone who asks of you. And from him who takes away your goods do not ask them back. And just as you want men to do to you, you also do to them likewise.
>
> But if you love those who love you, what credit is that to you? For even sinners love those who love them. And if you do good to those who do good to you, what credit is that to you? For even sinners do the same. And if you lend to those from whom you hope to receive back, what credit is that to you? For even sinners lend to sinners to receive as much back. But love your enemies, do good, and lend, hoping for nothing in return; and your reward will be great, and you will be sons of the Most High. For He is kind to the unthankful and evil. Therefore be merciful, just as your Father also is merciful.
>
> — Luke 6:27–36

5. Be filled with the Word.

The Word lives and comes alive in us. It makes us wise. It dwells in us richly because it produces good fruit when we live according to it. "Let the word of Christ dwell in you richly in all wisdom" (Colossians 3:16). Jesus is the Word. Be filled with Him. "And the Word became flesh and dwelt among us, and we beheld His glory, the glory as of the only begotten of the Father, full of grace and truth" (John 1:14).

The more we make reading God's Word part of our daily time with Him, the readier we are to respond like Jesus to any person or situation. The more we read His Word, the more we get to know Him, His character, and His heart. His Word truly is a lamp and a light to us.

> How sweet are Your words to my taste,
> Sweeter than honey to my mouth!
> Through Your precepts I get understanding;
> Therefore I hate every false way.
>
> Your word is a lamp to my feet
> And a light to my path.
>
> — Psalm 119:103–105

6. Be humble and a servant to all

Jesus was humble, and He loves humility and wants us to be humble toward one another. He dwells with those who are humble:

> For thus says the High and Lofty One
> Who inhabits eternity, whose name is Holy:
> "I dwell in the high and holy place,
> With him who has a contrite and humble spirit,
> To revive the spirit of the humble,
> And to revive the heart of the contrite ones."
>
> — Isaiah 57:15

> Let nothing be done through selfish ambition or conceit, but in lowliness of mind let each esteem others better than himself. Let each of you look out not only for his own interests, but also for the interests of others… Let this mind be in you which was also in Christ Jesus… He

humbled Himself and became obedient to the point of death, even the death of the cross.

— Philippians 2:3-5, 8

Jesus's whole purpose in coming to live among us on earth was to serve us in love, to the point of giving up His life for us to give salvation to all: "The Son of Man did not come to be served, but to serve, and to give His life a ransom for many" (Matthew 20:28). Jesus said true servants will be wherever He is, ready to serve in love: "If anyone serves Me, let him follow Me; and where I am, there My servant will be also. If anyone serves Me, him My Father will honor" (John 12:26). One of the greatest ways we can serve is to "heal the sick, cleanse the lepers, raise the dead, cast out demons. Freely you have received, freely give" (Matthew 10:8).

7. Lead others and fulfill the Great Commission.

Jesus fulfilled the Law and the Prophets through love, giving our need for a relationship with His Father preference over His desire to avoid an agonizing death. Jesus was kind and affectionate and an excellent example of preferring others before Himself. He and His disciples and apostles led the way and taught us to do this. "Be kindly affectionate to one another with brotherly love, in honor giving preference to one another" (Romans 12:10). As *proēgeomai* in Greek, preference means to go before and show the way as a leader.[3] Jesus wants us to prefer others, lead them, and also to "go into all the world and preach the gospel to every creature. He who believes and is baptized will be saved; but he who does not believe will be condemned. And these signs will follow those who believe: In My name they will cast out demons; they will speak with new tongues; they will take up serpents; and if they drink anything deadly, it will by no means hurt them; they will lay hands on the sick, and they will recover" (Mark 16:15–18).

Emulate Jesus for Breakthrough

Dear reader, when you emulate Jesus as His disciple and follow Him closely, He will bring you breakthrough!

Ask yourself:

— Can I think of some additional ways that I can emulate Jesus?

Notes

[1] "Emulate." Merriam-Webster.com. Accessed May 8, 2018. https://www.merriam-webster.com/dictionary/emulate.

[2] "H7453 - rea` - Strong's Hebrew Lexicon (ESV)." Blue Letter Bible. Accessed 8 May, 2018. https://www.blueletterbible.org//lang/lexicon/lexicon.cfm?Strongs=H7453&t=ESV.

[3] "G4285 - proēgeomai - Strong's Greek Lexicon (NKJV)." Blue Letter Bible. Accessed 20 Oct, 2018. https://www.blueletterbible.org//lang/lexicon/lexicon.cfm?Strongs=G4285&t=NKJV.

— 9 —
Sensitize Yourself to Holy Spirit

ROMANS 8:27

He who searches the hearts knows what the mind of the Spirit is.

P	**P**ursue God, your heavenly Father.
R	**R**est in God.
E	**E**mulate Jesus.
S	**Sensitize yourself to Holy Spirit.**
S	**S**tand firm in Christ.

Before we look at how to sensitize yourself to Holy Spirit, it is important to learn what He does and what some of His characteristics are. This will help you to be aware of His involvement in your life and to be sensitive to Him. Holy Spirit is your friend, and He wants you to know Him, talk with Him, hear Him, and follow Him. He is the Spirit of truth and will guide you into all truth; He will tell you what He hears from Father God and Jesus. The Holy Spirit helps you to have breakthrough.

Sensitize Yourself to Holy Spirit

What Holy Spirit does

Holy Spirit teaches you to do God's will—He leads you to do what is right in God's sight: "Teach me to do Your will, for You are my God; Your Spirit is good. Lead me in the land of uprightness" (Psalm 143:10). Holy Spirit helps you to walk according to God's Word: "I will put My Spirit within you and cause you to walk in My statutes, and you will keep My judgments and do them" (Ezekiel 36:27).

Holy Spirit empowers you: "So he answered and said to me: 'This is the word of the Lord to Zerubbabel: "Not by might nor by power, but by My Spirit," says the Lord of hosts'" (Zechariah 4:6). Holy Spirit guides you into all truth: "However, when He, the Spirit of truth, has come, He will guide you into all truth; for He will not speak on His own authority, but whatever He hears He will speak; and He will tell you things to come" (John 16:13). Holy Spirit intercedes for you: "Likewise the Spirit also helps in our weaknesses. For we do not know what we should pray for as we ought, but the Spirit Himself makes intercession for us with groanings which cannot be uttered. Now He who searches the hearts knows what the mind of the Spirit is, because He makes intercession for the saints according to the will of God" (Romans 8:26–27).

Holy Spirit helps you to walk in the Spirit: "I say then: Walk in the Spirit, and you shall not fulfill the lust of the flesh" (Galatians 5:16); "For as many as are led by the Spirit of God, these are sons of God. For you did not receive the spirit of bondage again to fear, but you received the Spirit of adoption by whom we cry out, 'Abba, Father'" (Romans 8:14–15). Holy Spirit communicates with you. He submits to Father God's authority and only speaks what He hears Father say, just as Jesus did while on earth and does so now. Holy Spirit will give you a nudge when you are tempted to sin, then you choose to sin or not. He will give you a nudge and tell you to not say or do something that will hurt you or someone else, then it is up to you to obey Him or not. He will tell you to say something that will bring you or others encouragement, joy, and more! He will prompt you to follow through on what you said you would do: "For those who live according to the flesh set their minds on the things of the flesh, but those who live according to the Spirit, the things of the Spirit" (Romans 8:5).

Holy Spirit gives you instructions: "The Holy Spirit said, 'Now separate to Me Barnabas and Saul for the work to which I have called them.' Then, having fasted and prayed, and laid hands on them, they sent them away" (Acts 13:2–3). Holy Spirit tells you what to say and not to say, as He did with Paul and Timothy: "Now when they had gone through Phrygia and the region of Galatia, they were forbidden by the Holy Spirit to preach the word in Asia" (Acts 16:6).

Holy Spirit helps you to hear what He is saying to you. "And I heard a voice saying to me, 'Rise, Peter; kill and eat'" (Acts 11:7). Holy Spirit tells you what to do and think. When Peter was visited by three men from Caesarea, the Spirit told Peter "to go with them, doubting nothing" (v. 12). Holy Spirit brings things to your remembrance, like the word of the Lord: Peter said, "Then I remembered the word of the Lord, how He said, 'John indeed baptized with water, but you shall be baptized with the Holy Spirit'" (v. 16).

Holy Spirit gives you power to speak with boldness: "'Now, Lord, look on their threats, and grant to Your servants that with all boldness they may speak Your word, by stretching out Your hand to heal, and that signs and wonders may be done through the name of Your holy Servant Jesus.' And when they had prayed, the place where they were assembled together was shaken; and they were all filled with the Holy Spirit, and they spoke the word of God with boldness" (Acts 4:29–31). Holy Spirit gives you visions. "I was in the city of Joppa praying; and in a trance I saw a vision, an object descending like a great sheet, let down from heaven by four corners; and it came to me" (Acts 11:5).

Characteristics of Holy Spirit

Holy Spirit is a gift from God. Peter said, "God gave them the same gift as He gave us when we believed on the Lord Jesus Christ" (Acts 11:17). Holy Spirit can be grieved. He is sorrowful when you do not follow Him. It is important to respect Him in your life as a gift from Father God and Jesus. He wants you to become familiar with and sensitive to what pleases Him and grieves Him. He wants fellowship with you because He loves you and cares for you. "And do not grieve the Holy Spirit of God, by whom you were sealed for the day of redemption" (Ephesians 4:30).

When you are sensitive to Holy Spirit, you can feel what hurts Him. Sometimes you may feel sadness, but you do not have anything to grieve about. You may feel that Holy Spirit is grieving about something that He wants you to pray for; it may be something in your own life or someone else's. When you follow Holy Spirit's leading, He can use your life to help many people and situations have breakthrough. There is great fulfillment in working and partnering with Him to accomplish His missions in the earth! Fellowshipping with Him will bring you great joy, and you and He will do mighty exploits for God!

Additionally, when you feel Holy Spirit grieving, it may be from some things that the enemy is targeting at you. Holy Spirit may want you to intercede, pray alone or with others, and enter into fellowship with Him as He protects you in the storm. Then, when the spiritual warfare is over, you will feel a release of oppression and enter into freedom. Holy Spirit may give you instructions on what to do and what not to do. He may give you a course correction and tell you to go in another direction. He may tell you to repent of something. He may tell you to rest in Him and more. He always protects you, comforts you, and stands in the gap for you. He is your *paraclete* which is "(1) a legal advocate, or counsel for defense, (2) an intercessor, (3) a helper, generally."[1] The Holy Spirit as *paraclete* is called to your side to be your aid, and He pleads your cause. He is your counsel of defense, your advocate, and helper. He leads you to a deeper knowledge of the gospel truth, and He gives you divine strength to undergo trials and persecution. He is your intercessor, consoler, and comforter, and He gives you relief.[2]

Holy Spirit is a gentleman. He will not force Himself on you. He gives you a free will to receive Him, just as Father God and Jesus do as well. Ask Him to help you throughout each day and night. He sees and knows everything. If you are lost and do not know how to get to where you are going, ask Him what to do and where to go, and He will tell you, show you, or guide someone to find you. If you lose something, ask Him where it is; He will show you, or He may send an angel to make what you lost appear again. If someone is asking you a question and you do not know the answer, ask Holy Spirit, and He will tell you what to say. He is your helper, friend, and counselor.

Ask yourself:

— Can I remember when Holy Spirit helped me to do something I felt I could not do on my own?

— Can I remember when Holy Spirit told me to not do something that could hurt me or others?

— Can I remember when Holy Spirit helped me to find something I lost, and this brought me peace?

— Can I remember when Holy Spirit helped me to remember something I needed to know, and this brought me peace?

SENSITIZE YOURSELF TO HOLY SPIRIT

Here are some ways that you can become sensitive to Holy Spirit:

1. Let go of pride and be humble.
2. Do not judge but discern with mercy.
3. Allow the Lord to change your heart.
4. Walk in forgiveness and repentance.
5. Have a fear of the Lord and not man.
6. Walk uprightly before the Lord.
7. Trust, trust, and trust again in the Lord.
8. Surrender to the Lord, and let His desires become your desires.

1. Let go of pride and be humble.

Pride is the opposite of humility. Pride says, I will do things my way because I know what is best. Humility recognizes and says, I will seek God and do things His way because He knows what is best.

It is said that pride comes before a fall:
Pride goes before destruction,
And a haughty spirit before a fall.
Better to be of a humble spirit with the lowly,
Than to divide the spoil with the proud.
— Proverbs 16:18–19

"God resists the proud, but gives grace to the humble." Therefore submit to God. . . . Draw near to God and He will draw near to you. . . . Purify your hearts, you double-minded. Lament and mourn and weep! . . . Humble yourselves in the sight of the Lord, and He will lift you up.
— James 4:6–10

SENSITIZE YOURSELF TO HOLY SPIRIT

When you humble yourself before God and He lifts you up, this does not mean that He exalts you or wants others to idolize you; it means that He will uplift your heart after you have repented of pride and mourned ways that you separated yourself from God—through self-exaltation and relying on your own strength and ways instead of His. "And whoever exalts himself will be humbled, and he who humbles himself will be exalted" (Matthew 23:12).

Ask the Holy Spirit to help you release your pride to Him and help you to be humble. The humbler you are, the more sensitive you will be to the Holy Spirit's leading. He will see that He can trust you with others, and He will increase your anointing, authority, and influence in people's lives, the world, and in God's kingdom.

God's Word instructs you to be honoring and humble, giving preference to your brothers and sisters, and to surround yourself with the humble. As you recall, the word *preference* means to lead, so God instructs you to lead others in His ways through humility: "Be kindly affectionate to one another with brotherly love, in honor giving preference to one another. . . . Rejoice with those who rejoice, and weep with those who weep. Be of the same mind toward one another. Do not set your mind on high things, but associate with the humble. Do not be wise in your own opinion" (Romans 12:10, 15–16).

AN EXAMPLE OF PRIDE

King Uzziah started out doing what was right in the sight of the Lord—the mark of a good king in the Old Testament. He was crowned king at the age of sixteen, and for years he asked God to lead and guide him during times of peace and war. He built up his army and led his people well until his fame and power went to his head. "His pride led to his downfall. He was unfaithful to the Lord his God, and entered the temple of the Lord to burn incense on the altar of incense" (2 Chronicles 26:16 NIV). The priests confronted him and told him God would no longer honor him: "Uzziah, who had a censer in his hand ready to burn incense, became angry. While he was raging at the priests in their presence before the incense altar in the Lord's temple, leprosy broke out on his forehead. . . . The Lord had afflicted him. King Uzziah had leprosy until the day he died. He lived in a separate house—leprous, and banned from the temple of the Lord. Jotham his son had charge of the palace and governed the people of the land" (vv. 19–21 NIV).

There are consequences for operating in pride. God corrects and disciplines those He loves. When you are prideful, you set yourself up as your own god and you enter into self-idolatry. You think more highly of yourself than you ought to and become arrogant. You think you are better than others, that you do not need anyone and you do not need God. God will not have any other gods before Him—not you, things, ideas, mind-sets, or other tangible and intangible items.

We must walk in humility: "By humility and the fear of the Lord are riches and honor and life" (Proverbs 22:4); "Be submissive to one another, and be clothed with humility, for 'God resists the proud, but gives grace to the humble.' Therefore humble yourselves under the mighty hand of God, that He may exalt you in due time" (1 Peter 5:5–6).

Our humility before God sensitizes us to see what He sees and to hear what He hears. Our humility attracts God, and He hears our prayers: "If My people who are called by My name will humble themselves, and pray and seek My face, and turn from their wicked ways, then I will hear from heaven, and will forgive their sin and heal their land. Now My eyes will be open and My ears attentive to prayer made in this place" (2 Chronicles 7:14–15); "Lord, You have heard the desire of the humble; You will prepare their heart" (Psalm 10:17).

2. Do not judge but discern with mercy.

You'll be judged with equal measure to the amount you judge others:

> Judge not, that you be not judged. For with what judgment you judge, you will be judged; and with the measure you use, it will be measured back to you. And why do you look at the speck in your brother's eye, but do not consider the plank in your own eye? Or how can you say to your brother, "Let me remove the speck from your eye"; and look, a plank is in your own eye? Hypocrite! First remove the plank from your own eye, and then you will see clearly to remove the speck from your brother's eye.
>
> — Matthew 7:1-5

Instead of judging others, ask God to help you recognize how people act out of their hurt and pain. Discern with mercy that they need help, and do not take their words, actions, or attacks personally. Pray for God to bring them healing and deliverance. Ask the Lord how to show His love to them, initiate conversation with them, and respond to them.

Watch what comes into your mind and out of your mouth when you think of others: "Humble yourselves in the sight of the Lord, and He will lift you up. Do not speak evil of one another, brethren. He who speaks evil of a brother and judges his brother, speaks evil of the law and judges the law. But if you judge the law, you are not a doer of the law but a judge. There is one Lawgiver, who is able to save and to destroy. Who are you to judge another?" (James 4:10-12).

Do not rely on your own thoughts and feelings, but seek God's heart, and find out what He says about a person, situation, or organization. Seek His truth. The more you know, absorb, and live in God's Word of truth and life, the more you will be able to discern the truth of a matter and the thoughts and intents of a person's heart: "For the word of God is living and powerful, and sharper than any two-edged sword, piercing even to the division of soul and spirit, and of joints and marrow, and is a discerner of the thoughts and intents of the heart" (Hebrews 4:12). God's Holy Spirit will tell you who and what you are dealing with underneath a persona, mask, or smokescreen. He will help you to know when a person is operating in or is influenced by the Holy Spirit of God or the human spirit—the carnal nature or Satan and his demons. Once you feel that the Holy Spirit has given you this information, then ask Him to confirm if you are truly hearing from Him. When you want only the truth, His truth, He will clarify it for you and give you a sense of knowing in your mind and spirit.

God has given you a good mind to do many things in the earth, but He does not want your mind to be your main source. He wants to be your main source. He wants you to submit your thoughts, feelings, and spirit to His Holy Spirit, so you will be led by Him and not your carnal, judgmental nature. As you do this throughout the day and night, you will be able to know what He is saying to you more and more.

Ask the Holy Spirit to give you discernment, grace, and mercy toward others. The more you are discerning and merciful toward others, the more sensitive you will be to the Holy Spirit's leading.

3. Allow the Lord to change your heart.

In order to live empowered by Holy Spirit, ask God to reveal your true heart. Ask Him to show you how to cleanse and heal your thoughts, emotions, and beliefs. He wants to put a mirror in front

SENSITIZE YOURSELF TO HOLY SPIRIT

of your heart and expose any dark, hidden, damaged parts of your heart from the effects of sin and pain in your life. He also wants to show you any ways that you agree with the enemy.

When you agree with the enemy, you walk in your carnal or fleshly nature. When you experience spiritual warfare from the enemy, he comes against your thoughts, emotions, body, and spirit. Ask God to help you to quickly notice when the enemy lies to you about yourself, God, and others, when he accuses you and puts you and others down. The enemy tries to convince you to stay and live in darkness, but you must decide daily to stay in close relationship with the Lord your God, walk in the Spirit, and not tolerate the enemy's tactics. Decide to believe the truth about how God sees you, who you are as His child, and your rights and privileges in His kingdom—according to His Word.

The Lord your God wants to remove your pain and give you a new heart. Years ago, the Lord showed me that from my growing-up years of experiencing a lot of abuse and neglect, I had a very tender, broken, cold, stony heart with walls of self-protection around it. He told me that He wanted to melt it and massage it and bring it back to life, and all I had to do was yield to His process of healing. I did this. It was scary and painful at first, but He was faithful to bring me great healing and breakthrough!

Ezekiel felt alone and abandoned because God had scattered His people across the nations on account of their sin, and Ezekiel was unsure if they would ever come back. But then God gave Ezekiel a promise: "'I will give you back the land of Israel again.' They will return to it and remove all its vile images and detestable idols. I will give them an undivided heart and put a new spirit in them; I will remove from them their heart of stone and give them a heart of flesh. Then they will follow my decrees and be careful to keep my laws. 'They will be my people, and I will be their God'" (Ezekiel 11:17–20 NIV). God knew that his people needed humble hearts and a strong relationship with Him if they were to flourish in the land He had given them.

You may feel that you have a good relationship with the Lord—you talk with Him, you follow Him the best you know how, and you love Him. But there may be some hurts in your heart from the past and present that cause you to be fearful and self-protective. You're putting up walls between you and others—and even God—without being aware of it. God wants all your heart. He wants you to give Him the pain you know about and the pain you do not know about (and may have forgotten and even forgiven, but it still causes you to hold back in some ways from God). Ask Him to give you a new heart. Don't presume that you are A-OK with God. Humble yourself, and submit your heart and mind to Him each day. You do not want anything to stand between you and your relationship with Him. You want to treasure it, nurture it, and be blessed in it! Ask Him to heal you and deliver you from all pain that keeps you from Him, even in the minutest way. He wants to heal you and bring you fulfillment and joy!

If your heart is hardened from pain, hurt, unforgiveness, pride, bitterness, and judgments from others toward you or from you to others and maybe toward God—because of pain and losses in your life—allow His Holy Spirit to bring these to the surface, expose them to His light, and let Him heal you. God will heal your broken heart because He loves you very much. When you ask Him to help you, you are saying, "God, I recognize you as the one and only one God in my life, and I need you. I trust you to heal and deliver me." He honors this greatly and He blesses you for trusting in Him. This pleases Him, and it warms His heart!

Dear reader, God is faithful to bring you breakthrough. Allow Him to sensitize you to Holy Spirit so you allow Him to be fully at work in your life. "For you were once darkness, but now you are light in the Lord. Walk as children of light (for the fruit of the

Spirit is in all goodness, righteousness, and truth)" (Ephesians 5:8–9). When you are sensitive to Him, He will use your life to help people. Ask Holy Spirit to help you to allow God to change your heart. The more you are flexible and pliable as He molds and shapes you, the more sensitive you will be to His leading. "You are our Father; we are the clay, and You our potter; and all we are the work of Your hand" (Isaiah 64:8).

4. Walk in forgiveness and repentance.

It is important to disclose the truth of your sin to God. Even though He already knows it, He wants you to confess it to Him and talk with Him about it. He is relational, and He loves you. He wants you to relate to Him and have conversations with Him. He knows that you are human and imperfect; He does not expect you to be perfect. Only Jesus is perfect. He knows that sometimes you sin, but when you ask Him to forgive you, He will. He just asks that you forgive those who have hurt you as well. I believe one of the greatest supernatural miracles that God gives to mankind is forgiveness of sin.

> For if you forgive men their trespasses, your heavenly Father will also forgive you. But if you do not forgive men their trespasses, neither will your Father forgive your trespasses.
>
> — Matthew 6:14-15

> Therefore be merciful, just as your Father also is merciful. Judge not, and you shall not be judged. Condemn not, and you shall not be condemned. Forgive, and you will be forgiven.

> Give, and it will be given to you: good measure, pressed down, shaken together, and running over will be put into

your bosom. For with the same measure that you use, it will be measured back to you.

—Luke 6:36–38

Dear reader, please receive His grace and mercy that He gives to you freely through Jesus's death and resurrection. Do not receive any condemnation of false guilt or false accusations from the enemy after God has forgiven you. Even if you feel that you need to ask God for forgiveness a hundred times a day for different things, give yourself grace and do not punish yourself. Jesus already became the punishment for your sin: "Now, once at the end of the ages, He has appeared to put away sin by the sacrifice of Himself" (Hebrews 9:26). The Lord wants you to receive His forgiveness and walk in freedom with Him.

The Lord your God wants you to repent—to be truly sorry for your sin. He wants you to recognize that you sinned not only against man but against God, first and foremost. He wants you to see that you caused Him (plus Jesus and Holy Spirit), yourself, and maybe others pain. He wants you to have a contrite (sorrowful) heart about your sin and to ask Him to help you to overcome and have breakthrough. When King David sinned, he repented and acknowledged to God, "Against You, You only, have I sinned, and done this evil in Your sight— that You may be found just when You speak, and blameless when You judge" (Psalm 51:4). Repentance means you acknowledge that you have sinned, and you make an effort to change from your ways and turn and go in God's good direction for you. He always wants the best for you! He wants to help you not cause pain to yourself and others. Keep your heart tender before Him. Ask Him to help you to avoid sin and He will. When you want to avoid the pain of sin toward Father God, yourself, and others, you will develop a closer relationship with Him, Jesus, and Holy Spirit.

SENSITIZE YOURSELF TO HOLY SPIRIT

Ask Holy Spirit to help you to become sensitive to His presence in your life. The more sensitive you become to the Holy Spirit, the quicker you will recognize your sin and ask for forgiveness, and the quicker you will feel the conviction, direction, and empowerment of the Holy Spirit to not sin.

Also, be willing to receive ministry from those who love God and will pray for you and counsel you. Receive healing and deliverance from the Lord for the hurts and disappointments in your life. This can help you to forgive others, yourself, and God, if needed. This can also help you to repent, receive forgiveness from God, and walk uprightly before Him.

Operate in the opposite spirit, which is the Holy Spirit. Joseph chose to operate in the opposite spirit from his brothers'—one of jealousy, hate, and murder (Genesis 37:3-5, 18-20). Joseph chose to allow Holy Spirit to operate through him. He decided to forgive, love, protect, and provide for his brothers and family, just like Father God, Jesus, and Holy Spirit do for you (Genesis 50:15-21; 47:11-12). "If your enemy is hungry, give him bread to eat; and if he is thirsty, give him water to drink; for so you will heap coals of fire on his head, and the Lord will reward you" (Proverbs 25:21-22). By doing this you diffuse and annihilate Satan's influence in your life. He loses his power against you and those you influence.

God's Word teaches you to walk in the Spirit, not in your carnal nature that fulfills the desires of your flesh. If you respond to hurts in your carnal nature with anger, retaliation, and the like, you end up operating in a contrary spirit to God's Holy Spirit. You participate with the enemy and come under his condemnation, which can draw you away from God. It is important to recognize this and break the enemy's hold on you. Forgive and operate in the Holy Spirit, and respond to people, organizations, and others with the fruit of the Spirit: "The fruit of the Spirit is love, joy, peace, longsuffering, kindness, goodness, faithfulness, gentleness, self-control" (Galatians 5:22–23). Ask God to help you to take the seeds of your fruit and the lessons that you learned in following Him and plant them in others' lives—to see them grow and mature in Him. Then He will help them to plant new seeds from their fruit into others' lives and see them grow and mature as well.

Dear reader, ask the Holy Spirit to help you to walk in forgiveness toward others, yourself, and God, and ask for forgiveness when you sin against God and man. The more you walk in forgiveness, the more sensitive you will be to the Holy Spirit's leading.

5. Have a fear of the Lord and not man.

God wants you to not fear man or circumstances but to fear Him. To *fear* Him means to revere, respect, honor, and be in awe of Him. Honor His majesty, greatness, and love for you. "Let all the earth fear the Lord; let all the inhabitants of the world stand in awe of Him" (Psalm 33:8). God is your strength! To fear the Lord also means to want to please Him and have Him first in your life. If you do things to please yourself first, you are not allowing God to do His job in protecting and leading you. You become the driver, and you can miss many things that He wants for you. You can get detoured and lost. It is important for you to partner with Him by seeking what He wants for you and then following His lead.

If you do things to please others first rather than God first, you can lose your identity in who you are in Christ. This means that you will become what another person wants you to be rather than who God has called you to be. So let go of any striving to perform or please man for approval to gain your sense of worth and identity. Seek to please the Lord your God first. "The fear of the Lord is the beginning of wisdom; a good understanding have all those who do His commandments. His praise endures forever"

(Psalm 111:10). [Please see Appendix F for Scriptures on your identity, who you are in Christ.]

God gives you freedom and grace to choose many things and the choice to please others and bring them joy but not at the expense of Him losing first place in your life. When you honor Him and love Him, you trust that He will protect you, lead you, and give you the best in every area of your life. "The angel of the Lord encamps all around those who fear Him, and delivers them" (Psalm 34:7). When you fear the Lord and want to please Him first and foremost, He knows that He can trust you with information and responsibilities that are very important to Him. "The Lord confides in those who fear him; he makes his covenant known to them" (Psalm 25:14 NIV). He will help you to live a fulfilling life, and He will give you breakthrough!

6. Walk uprightly before the Lord.

Psalm 15:2 says the person who can dwell on His holy hill is "he who walks uprightly, and works righteousness, and speaks the truth in his heart." *Uprightly* means whole, complete, full, sound, healthful, unimpaired, innocent, having integrity, entirely in accord with truth and fact.[3] The Lord your God helps you to walk uprightly before Him. He helps you to be complete and walk entirely in accord with His truth. "For the Lord God is a sun and shield; the Lord will give grace and glory; no good thing will He withhold from those who walk uprightly" (Psalm 84:11).

Ask the Holy Spirit to help you to have a fear of the Lord, not man, and to walk uprightly before Him. "Folly is joy to him who is destitute of discernment, but a man of understanding walks uprightly" (Proverbs 15:21). The more you have a fear of the Lord and not man and walk uprightly before God, the more sensitive you will be to the Holy Spirit's leading. "He who walks righteously and speaks uprightly, . . . he will dwell on high; his place of defense will be the fortress of rocks; bread will be given him, his water will be sure" (Isaiah 33:15-16).

7. Trust, trust, and trust again in the Lord.

Be willing to let go of any fears and control, and trust in the Lord your God. Hear Him, and follow His good path on which He walks hand in hand with you. Give him every fear and concern, and wait on Him. He will come through for you and bless your obedience and trust in Him!

Father God's logic and understanding are more profound than yours: "'For My thoughts are not your thoughts, nor are your ways My ways,' says the Lord. 'For as the heavens are higher than the earth, so are My ways higher than your ways, and My thoughts than your thoughts'" (Isaiah 55:8-9). Trust Him. Ask Him to help you to know His thoughts and His ways, so you will have understanding and not rely on your own mind but rather on the Holy Spirit. Have faith in His ability to help you. Have faith in your willingness to follow Him and apply the mind of Christ that Jesus gave to you "Blessed is the man who trusts in the Lord, and whose hope is the Lord. For he shall be like a tree planted by the waters, which spreads out its roots by the river, and will not fear when heat comes; but its leaf will be green, and will not be anxious in the year of drought, nor will cease from yielding fruit" (Jeremiah 17:7-8).

When you trust in the Lord, you believe in His love for you and you believe in His goodness toward you. You do not doubt Him; you fully trust and believe in Him, His Word, His will, and His ways. You know that only goodness and life will come from your following Him. Therefore, be willing to follow Him 100 percent. It is like having faith as a little child in Him and His goodness:

> Unless you repent [that is, change your inner self—your old way of thinking, live changed lives] and become like children [trusting, humble, and forgiving], you will never enter the kingdom of heaven. Therefore, whoever humbles himself like this child is greatest in the kingdom of heaven.
>
> — Matthew 18:2-4 AMP

> Whoever does not receive the kingdom of God [with faith and humility] like a child will not enter it at all.
>
> — Luke 18:17 AMP

You can trust Father God. "He is a shield to all who trust in Him" (2 Samuel 22:31). He does not forsake those who seek Him and know His name (Psalm 9:10). God is your strength and song, your salvation. You can choose to "trust and not be afraid" (Isaiah 12:2), just as the disciples and apostles did many times. "We were burdened beyond measure, above strength, so that we despaired even of life. Yes, we had the sentence of death in ourselves, that we should not trust in ourselves but in God who raises the dead, who delivered us from so great a death, and does deliver us; in whom we trust that He will still deliver us" (2 Corinthians 1:8-10).

Dear reader, ask the Holy Spirit to help you to trust in Him, your Father God, and Jesus, His Son. The more you trust in Him, the more sensitive you will be to the Holy Spirit's leading.

8. Surrender to the Lord, and let His desires become your desires.

Be humble in your desires and surrender them to Him. God knows your wants and needs. He wants to take very good care of you and bless you with your desires, prayers, and petitions. But also consider asking God to help His desires for your life to become your desires. For He knows you better than you know yourself.

Sensitize Yourself to Holy Spirit

Trust that He will even give you desires that you have not thought of, thoughts that will bring you in to more fullness of life than you could have done with your own desires. "Trust in the Lord, and do good; dwell in the land, and feed on His faithfulness. Delight yourself also in the Lord, and He shall give you the desires of your heart. Commit your way to the Lord, trust also in Him, and He shall bring it to pass" (Psalm 37:3-5).

Desire God's will for your life, and you will be blessed, for He always knows and wants what is best for you. Ask Holy Spirit to teach you God's will in all situations, and how to do God's will, and He will! King David was a man after God's own heart because when he fell, he got back up and he persevered; he would not let go of God. He desired to do God's will, and he wanted to please Him. He loved to praise and worship God, and he was repentant when he sinned.

What you think on is what you will desire. What you desire is what you will think on. So think on and request from God what is good, holy, and pure: "Whatever things are true, whatever things are noble, whatever things are just, whatever things are pure, whatever things are lovely, whatever things are of good report, if there is any virtue and if there is anything praiseworthy—meditate on these things" (Philippians 4:8). Meditating on Psalm 34 can also help you to become sensitive to God's Holy Spirit.

Dear reader, ask the Holy Spirit to help you to surrender to Him, Father God, and Jesus, His Son, and for His desires to become your desires. The more you do this, the more sensitive you will be to the Holy Spirit's leading.

NOTES

[1] "Paraclete." Bible Study Tools. Accessed 30 Jun, 2018. https://www.biblestudytools.com/dictionary/paraclete/.

[2] "G3875 - paraklētos – Strong's Greek Lexicon (NKJV)." Blue Letter Bible. Accessed 30 Jun, 2018. https://www.blueletterbible.org//lang/lexicon/lexicon.cfm?Strongs=G3875&t=NKJV.

[3] "H8549 - tamiym – Strong's Hebrew Lexicon (NKJV)." Blue Letter Bible. Accessed 4 Jun, 2018. https://www.blueletterbible.org//lang/lexicon/lexicon.cfm?Strongs=H8549&t=NKJV.

— 10 —
Stand Firm in Christ

PROVERBS 10:25 NIV

When the storm has swept by, the wicked are gone, but the righteous stand firm forever.

P	**P**ursue God, your heavenly Father.
R	**R**est in God.
E	**E**mulate Jesus.
S	**S**ensitize yourself to Holy Spirit.
S	**Stand firm in Christ.**

I love God's meaning of the words *stand firm*—"stand strong." When the enemy tries to detour you, discourage you, and more, God wants you to look to Him, hold on to Him, and get right back up. "My dear brothers and sisters, stand firm. Let nothing move you. Always give yourselves fully to the work of the Lord, because you know that your labor in the Lord is not in vain" (1 Corinthians 15:58 NIV). When everything goes awry, and you feel spiritual warfare from the enemy, do not compromise, don't give up, and don't give in to him. Stand strong and firm in God's living Word, and believe what He says, no matter what your circumstances look like and no matter how you feel, and He will give you breakthrough! "You will be hated by everyone because of me, but the one who stands firm to the end will be saved" (Matthew 10:22 NIV).

It is important to examine the motives of your heart so they will be pure, simple, and of God. I call it doing a personal inventory of your heart. "Be obedient . . . not with eye service, as men-pleasers, but as bondservants of Christ, doing the will of God from the heart, with goodwill doing service, as to the Lord, and not to men" (Ephesians 6:5–7). God wants you to have a pure heart that is surrendered to Him. He wants you to know, through His Word, what pleases Him, and He wants you to follow Him. He blesses you and rewards you when you do this. "Without faith it is impossible to please Him, for he who comes to God must believe that He is, and that He is a rewarder of those who diligently seek Him" (Hebrews 11:6).

Your feelings are fleeting; they can go up and down and come and go. It is important for you to be saturated with the truth of God's Word in your mind and heart so you will recognize when the enemy lies to you and how his lies affect your emotions and thoughts. "It is for freedom that Christ has set us free. Stand firm, then, and do not let yourselves be burdened again by a yoke of slavery" (Galatians 5:1 NIV). When you do this, you will be steadfast, unmovable, and stand firm in your beliefs in God and your convictions of righteousness and truth. You will be unalterable in the face of any adversity! You will only be moved and changed by the Lord, hallelujah! You will be flexible and pliable in His hands. "Be patient and stand firm, because the Lord's coming is near" (James 5:8 NIV). When you feel weak, remember Jesus is strong in you.

When You Are Weak, He Is Strong

When you walk with the Lord, He lives in you by the power of Holy Spirit who gives you strength and breakthrough! Isn't it a relief to know that you do not have to be strong in yourself or through your own efforts? Rest in Jesus, and allow His strength and power to rest in you. "'My grace is sufficient for you, for my power is made perfect in weakness.' Therefore I will boast all the more gladly about my weaknesses, so that Christ's power may rest on me" (2 Corinthians 12:9-10 NIV). Allow Him and His Word of life to live in and through you. He asks you to abide in Him the way a branch abides in and is connected to a vine—to receive the nourishment, strength, and life that help it bear fruit that will remain: "If you abide in Me, and My words abide in you, you will ask what you desire, and it shall be done for you. By this My Father is glorified, that you bear much fruit; so you will be My disciples. . . . You did not choose Me, but I chose you and appointed you that you should go and bear fruit, and that your fruit should remain" (John 15:7-8, 16).

You cannot stand firm when you have been knocked out and you're still lying on the ground. "When the storm has swept by, the wicked are gone, but the righteous stand firm forever" (Proverbs 10:25 NIV). You must look to the Lord, receive His powerful love for you, and get up and persevere. Even if you cannot get up physically, get up in your spirit. Rise up and believe in Him and with Him for your breakthrough! Remember that He is faithful, and as you press through, He will bring you breakthrough. "We work with you for your joy, because it is by faith you stand firm" (2 Corinthians 1:24 NIV). Ask friends to help pray your way through to breakthrough, just as Epaphras did for the Colossian believers: "Epaphras, who is one of you and a servant of Christ Jesus, sends greetings. He is always wrestling in prayer for you, that you may stand firm in all the will of God, mature and fully assured" (Colossians 4:12 NIV).

> Finally, be strong in the Lord and in his mighty power. Put on the full armor of God, so that you can take your stand against the devil's schemes. For our struggle is not against flesh and blood, but against the rulers, against the authorities, against the powers of this dark world and against the spiritual forces of evil in the heavenly realms. Therefore put on the full armor of God, so that when the day of evil comes, you may be able to stand your ground, and after you have done everything, to stand. Stand firm then, with the belt of truth buckled around your waist, with the breastplate of righteousness in place, and with your feet fitted with the readiness that comes from the gospel of peace. In addition to all this, take up the shield of faith, with which you can extinguish all the flaming arrows of the evil one. Take the helmet of salvation and the sword of the Spirit, which is the word of God. And pray in the Spirit on all occasions with all kinds of prayers and requests. With this in mind, be alert and always keep on praying for all the Lord's people.
>
> — Ephesians 6:10–18 NIV

Dear reader, God has far more resources and gifts He wants to bless you with than you can develop on your own. He wants you to look to Him, rely on Him, depend on Him, and have a close relationship with Him. Ask Him to help you to press through for breakthrough. As you do this, have faith in Him, love Him, and seek His will. Also, listen to Him, trust Him, obey Him, wait on Him, and do His will. Walk closely with Him through it all, for His love for you is great and everlasting, and His rewards for you are wonderful! Please receive His deep love and Holy Spirit's empowerment in your life today. He so desires to help you. Love Him and follow Him, and He will give you breakthrough in Him!

Pursue God, your heavenly Father, rest in God, emulate Jesus, sensitize yourself to Holy Spirit, and stand firm in Christ.

As you do this, and as you also allow Him to press into your life to bring forth the rich oil of His Holy Spirit, He will give you breakthrough! "For I am persuaded that neither death nor life, nor angels nor principalities nor powers, nor things present nor things to come, nor height nor depth, nor any other created thing, shall be able to separate us from the love of God which is in Christ Jesus our Lord" (Romans 8:38-39).

Ask yourself:

- What are some of the things I am working on to keep myself close to the Lord?
- What are some things I am doing to bless the Lord, His kingdom, and His church?
- Will I continue to serve Him and stand firm in His strength?
- What are some of the ways that He wants me to stand firm in my faith in Him?

III. Biblical Breakthrough

— 11 —
When Jesus and Bible Heroes Pressed Through

JOHN 17:4

> *I have finished the work which You have given Me to do.*

JESUS

Jesus Christ is the only begotten Son of God, the Savior of the world, the Lamb of God, God incarnate, Messiah, Anointed One, Messianic Prince, the King of Israel, the High Priest of Israel, Prophet, Chosen One, Elect (of God), King of Kings, and Lord of Lords! Father God wanted His only begotten Son, Jesus Christ, to pursue Him and press through for breakthrough to bless the people of this world who so desperately need His love and salvation.

Jesus pursued God as He pressed through for breakthrough. He chose to:

1. Have faith and believe that God loved Him, wanted a relationship with Him, and had a great plan for His life;
2. Seek God's will;

3. Listen to God;
4. Trust God, obey Him, wait on Him, and believe that He would bring Him breakthrough;
5. Do God's will at all costs, no matter what the circumstances looked like and felt like.

Everything that Jesus did is worthy of study and praise. He was and is always faithful in pursuing His Father, God. In regard to all that Jesus did while He lived on earth, the apostle John said, "And there are also many other things that Jesus did, which if they were written one by one, I suppose that even the world itself could not contain the books that would be written. Amen" (John 21:25).

JESUS PRESSED THROUGH FOR BREAKTHROUGH IN THE DESERT

Jesus knows what it feels like when you go through the pressing process. He knows what it is like for you to be in the wilderness—the dry desert experiences of life. He knows what it is like to be tempted by the devil. Jesus pursued God in every area of his life, all throughout His life. He pursued God before He began His ministry and when He was tempted in the wilderness, and He won the victory!

> But He answered and said, "It is written, 'Man shall not live by bread alone, but by every word that proceeds from the mouth of God.'" Then the devil took Him up into the holy city, set Him on the pinnacle of the temple, and said to Him, "If You are the Son of God, throw Yourself down. For it is written: 'He shall give His angels charge over you,' and, 'In their hands they shall bear you up, lest you dash your foot against a stone.'" Jesus said to him, "It is written again, 'You shall not tempt the Lord your God.'"

Again, the devil took Him up on an exceedingly high mountain, and showed Him all the kingdoms of the world and their glory. And he said to Him, "All these things I will give You if You will fall down and worship me." Then Jesus said to him, "Away with you, Satan! For it is written, 'You shall worship the Lord your God, and Him only you shall serve.'" Then the devil left Him, and behold, angels came and ministered to Him.

— Matthew 4:4–11

Jesus also won the victory over death when He died on the cross to take away the sins of the world. "For God so loved the world that He gave His only begotten Son, that whoever believes in Him should not perish but have everlasting life" (John 3:16). He has empowered you with His Holy Spirit—who lives in you—to help you face and overcome every adversity, test, trial, tribulation, and temptation. He guides you to victory and breakthrough! He loves you, and He is on your side!

Jesus went to the desert to press into God and to endure a pressing from God to prepare Him for His ministry. He needed to do this so He would stand, and having done all, to stand against every onslaught of the enemy. He pressed into His heavenly Father and allowed His heavenly Father to press on Him to bring forth His rich oil of gladness, the oil of joy that would bring His light into the whole earth and redeem mankind back into relationship with His heavenly Father!

JESUS PRESSED THROUGH FOR BREAKTHROUGH IN THE GARDEN OF GETHSEMANE

As noted in chapter 1, Jesus pursued God, obeyed Him, and endured a pressing on His life in the garden of Gethsemane. Jesus prayed in the garden of Gethsemane before His arrest for His disciples and those who would believe in Him through their message.

> Jesus spoke these words, lifted up His eyes to heaven, and said: "Father, the hour has come. . . . I have finished the work which You have given Me to do. . . . I have given to them the words which You have given Me. . . . I pray for them. . . . I kept them in Your name. . . . As You sent Me into the world, I also have sent them into the world. And for their sakes I sanctify Myself, that they also may be sanctified by the truth."
>
> — John 17:1, 4, 8-9, 12,18-19

Jesus wanted only His Father's will to be done at all costs, no matter what the circumstances. He was willing to press into God, seek His will, listen to Him, and obey Him because He loves God and He loves you. He knew God's plan was the best plan. Jesus had to let go of His own plans, desires, opinions, and will—long before He ever went to the cross—so that God's vision and plan would come to pass. Yet on the cross, Jesus felt every pain, sickness, disease, mental and physical torment, and spiritual pain man had ever and would ever experience on earth. He became a living sacrifice to break the curse of death and sickness once and for all.

Jesus redeemed you from death to life by pressing through. He made it possible for you to have relationship with your Father God and to never be separated from Him again, as Adam and Eve and all creation were after the fall of man (Genesis).

In His love and obedience to Father God, Jesus climbed Golgotha's hill to be crucified. He trusted in His Father God as He took every agonizing and painful step. Through the pressing processes and narrow walk of life with God, Jesus submitted to Father God and learned obedience from all that He suffered. Jesus pressed through and experienced breakthrough for you and all mankind! "During the days of Jesus's life on earth, he offered up prayers and petitions with fervent cries and tears to the one who could save him from death, and he was heard because of his reverent submission. Son though he was, he learned obedience from what he suffered and, once made perfect, he became the source of eternal salvation for all who obey him" (Hebrews 5:7–9 NIV).

Jesus pursued God as He pressed through for breakthrough and obeyed so that He (one Man, Jesus) could remove the condemnation of sin and death brought upon mankind (by one man, Adam) so you and all who believe on Him as Lord and Savior, and who obey Him, would not have eternal death but live forever with Him. "Just as through one man's disobedience [his failure to hear, his carelessness] the many were made sinners, so through the obedience of the one Man the many will be made righteous and acceptable to God and brought into right standing with Him" (Romans 5:19 AMP).

Jesus has justified you and made you righteous by His blood sacrifice on the cross. "There is therefore now no condemnation to those who are in Christ Jesus, who do not walk according to the flesh, but according to the Spirit. For the law of the Spirit of life in Christ Jesus has made me free from the law of sin and death" (Romans 8:1–2). When the enemy lies to you and tries to put condemnation on you and tell you that you are wrong, you are bad, and you are not this or that and that you are this and that, stand firm in your faith and tell him to back off—for you belong to the Lord. "For there stood by me this night an angel of the God to whom I *belong* and whom I serve" (Acts 27:23, emphasis mine).

YOU BELONG TO THE LORD

Dear reader, your Father God truly can and will fulfill your need for love, peace, joy, and all other needs. As you recognize God's greatness and what Jesus did for you on the cross, then surrender to Him daily. As you recognize that He sent Holy Spirit to live in you to teach you all things and to comfort you, then surrender to Him daily.

Recognize that you belong to the Lord, for He gave His life to give you new life in Him, now and eternally: "Do you not know that your body is the temple of the Holy Spirit who is in you, whom you have from God, and you are not your own? For you were bought at a price; therefore glorify God in your body and in your spirit, which are God's" (1 Corinthians 6:19–20).

He calls you to follow Him and live for Him, because in Him you find the true fulfillment you seek. Did you know that other people's lives depend on your following God's will? You influence people by your words and actions, even when you may not be aware of it. When you live for Christ, you shine His light and love to others. You help to bring new life—His life—to them. "You are the light of the world. A city that is set on a hill cannot be hidden. Nor do they light a lamp and put it under a basket, but on a lampstand, and it gives light to all who are in the house. Let your light so shine before men, that they may see your good works and glorify your Father in heaven (Matthew 5:14–16).

The Lord your God has a wonderful life for you—a greater, more adventurous, and fulfilling life than you can imagine. He wants to develop your gifts, talents, and callings. Press into Him and believe Him to bring you breakthrough for good change, healing, deliverance from problems, and more! He has very interesting people who need to know you; they need to be exposed to your gifts, talents, and love. And you need them because God is a relationship-based God. Everything He accomplishes in His kingdom has to do with relationships. Seek relationships with those who love Him and who demonstrate their love to you.

Ask yourself:

— Is the devil trying to tempt me in my life to agree with him in thoughts and actions and to not follow the Lord my God?

— Is the devil trying to get me to worship someone or something—even my own ideas, opinions, judgments, and anything other than the Lord my God?

— Will I press into Jesus and allow Him to bring forth the rich oil of His Holy Spirit in my life, so I can be a light of the world to help them see the one true God?

— Will I ask God to give me courage to hold onto Him and do His will, even when it is difficult?

— Will I submit to God's ways and His will and obey Him in pressing times?

BIBLE HEROES

God is very pleased when you pursue Him and allow His pressing process upon your life. All of the Bible heroes noted below pursued God as they pressed through for breakthrough. God wanted them to pursue Him, follow His will, press into Him, and allow His pressing process upon their lives so His rich oil could come through their lives to bless them, God, and others.

All Bible heroes chose to:

1. Have faith and believe that God loved them, wanted a relationship with them, and had a great plan for their lives;
2. Seek God's will;
3. Listen to God;
4. Trust God, obey Him, wait on Him, and believe that He would bring them breakthrough;

5. Do God's will at all costs, no matter what the circumstances looked like or felt like.

NOAH

Noah pursued God as he pressed through for breakthrough.

> Then the Lord saw that the wickedness of man was great in the earth, and that every intent of the thoughts of his heart was only evil continually. And the Lord was sorry that He had made man on the earth, and He was grieved in His heart. So the Lord said, "I will destroy man whom I have created from the face of the earth, both man and beast, creeping thing and birds of the air, for I am sorry that I have made them." But Noah found grace in the eyes of the Lord. ... Noah was a just man, perfect in his generations. Noah walked with God. ... And Noah did according to all that the Lord commanded him.
>
> — Genesis 6:5–9; 7:5

Noah had to press through with great faith in God to see breakthrough. He made a choice to believe, obey, and follow Him. He pursued God as he was building the ark for over one hundred years. He endured ridicule and scorn. He was steadfast. He persevered in his pursuit of God, being in God's will, and obeying God's voice. He had to keep working to build the ark to the exact dimensions God told him.

Noah had to get out of his comfort zone and live his life according to God's plan while not knowing what to expect in the future. Never knowing what rain was since it had never rained before, Noah had to keep on sawing and hammering that wood. His life was a yielded vessel fit for the Master's use for the salvation of mankind. I think one of the reasons it took Noah so long to build the ark is because God was working on Noah as Noah was working on the ark. Noah yielded his vessel—his life—to God as Noah was building God's vessel.

Dear reader, you can be a yielded vessel for honor, sanctified, useful to the Lord, and prepared for every good work so He can use your life to bless others. "If anyone cleanses himself from the latter (dishonor), he will be a vessel for honor, sanctified and useful for the Master, prepared for every good work" (2 Timothy 2:21). His will is, and always has been, to redeem us to His heavenly Father so we can know Him and live with Him forever. He does not want any of His children to be lost and separated from Him; this grieves Him. He loves His family, and He wants us all to feel and know His love.

The Bible said, Noah "found favor with God" and he "did according to all that the Lord commanded him." Noah pursued Father God, and He was in unity with Father God.

Just as God chose Noah to do a specific task, God chooses you to do specific tasks for Him because He has created you uniquely to accomplish them. As God pursues you to complete the assignments He has ordained for you to accomplish, will you say,

Yes, Father God, at all costs, no matter what the circumstances, I will be your yielded vessel. I recognize many lives are dependent on my obedience.

As those floodwaters broke through the heavens, Noah experienced breakthrough! He saw why God called him to build the ark, and he saw how his obedience to God saved mankind. Noah pursued God as he pressed through for breakthrough.

Ask yourself:

— Will I press into Jesus and allow Him to bring forth the rich oil of His Holy Spirit in my life, so I can be a light of the world to help them see the one true God?

- Will I be a vessel of honor for God so that He may use my life for His glory?
- Will I trust in His will, His ways, and His timing for me?
- Am I pursuing Him today?
- Will I allow God to prepare me for every good work to bless others, even when I don't understand the circumstances or know the outcome?

Press into God and He will bring you breakthrough!

Nehemiah

Nehemiah pursued God as he pressed through for breakthrough.

When Nehemiah heard that the Israelites who survived the exile were back in Jerusalem, and its city walls were broken down, he immediately pursued God for His direction and plan. While rebuilding the wall of Jerusalem, Nehemiah pursued the plan of God amid adversity, ridicule, and threats of war against him and the Israelites. Nehemiah did what God put on his heart for Jerusalem by rebuilding its wall of protection:

> They said to me, "Those who survived the exile and are back in the province are in great trouble and disgrace. The wall of Jerusalem is broken down, and its gates have been burned with fire." When I heard these things, I sat down and wept. For some days I mourned and fasted and prayed before the God of heaven. . . . I went to Jerusalem, and after staying there three days I set out during the night with a few others. I had not told anyone what my God had put in my heart to do for Jerusalem. . . . Then I said to them, "You see the trouble we are in: Jerusalem lies in ruins, and its gates have been burned with fire. Come, let us rebuild the wall of Jerusalem, and we will no longer be in disgrace." I also told them about the gracious hand

of my God on me and what the king had said to me. They replied, "Let us start rebuilding."

—Nehemiah 1:3-4; 2:11-12, 17-18 NIV

Are you ready to pray for people's protection and help rebuild their lives as they walk closely with God? Your prayers for them help close the gaps (openings) to the enemy and help build a wall of protection in their lives as you stand in the gap. "You have not gone up into the gaps to build a wall for the house of Israel to stand in battle on the day of the Lord. . . . So I sought for a man among them who would make a wall, and stand in the gap before Me on behalf of the land, that I should not destroy it; but I found no one" (Ezekiel 13:5; 22:30).

"When Sanballat, Tobiah, the Arabs, the Ammonites and the men of Ashdod heard that the repairs to Jerusalem's walls had gone ahead and that *the gaps were being closed*, they were very angry. They all plotted together to come and fight against Jerusalem and stir up trouble against it" (Nehemiah 4:7-8 NIV, emphasis mine). Their enemies continued to oppose them as they were rebuilding. "But we prayed to our God and posted a guard day and night to meet this threat" (v. 9).

As God rebuilds your life, do you feel the enemy opposing you, your family, your finances, your healing, and your breakthrough? Is the devil trying to keep your growth stunted and keep you unprotected? Is he trying to keep you from agreeing with God's will for your life? Well, God your heavenly Father is fighting for you! If you press in and keep believing, seeking, listening, trusting, and obeying Him, you will see your deliverance come to pass—for you and those you pray for. You will experience breakthrough!

The people of Judah were rebuilding the wall, and they were prepared for the enemies' attacks. "The officers posted themselves behind all the people of Judah who were building the wall. Those who carried materials did their work with one hand and held a weapon in the other, and each of the builders wore his sword at his side as he worked" (Nehemiah 4:16–18 NIV). They worked in unity with each other and with God, and they believed that God was fighting for them (v. 20). They even had a plan should anyone attack. "Wherever you hear the sound of the trumpet, join us there. Our God will fight for us!" (v. 20).

God is saying to you: *Come follow Me and My plan for your life. When you hear My trumpet call (My voice), come join Me. I will fight for you!* If your father, mother, brother, or sister was not there for you when you needed someone to fight for you, I tell you today that your Father God is fighting for you! He will bring your breakthrough, and He will protect you!

Nehemiah and the Israelites pursued God as they pressed through for breakthrough. And after the wall was rebuilt, Nehemiah gathered all the people together in unity, and they worshiped the Lord. They knew who had brought them their breakthrough (Nehemiah 9:5–6).

ABRAHAM

Abraham pursued God as he pressed through for breakthrough.

The Lord God called Abraham to go to the land where he would receive his inheritance. Before God changed his name to Abraham, He called him Abram. "Now the Lord had said to Abram: 'Get out of your country, from your family and from your father's house, to a land that I will show you'" (Genesis 12:1). "By faith Abraham obeyed when he was called to go out to the place which he would receive as an inheritance. And he went out, not knowing where he was going" (Hebrews 11:8). Abram trusted in the Lord.

Abram pressed through for breakthrough with great faith as God called him to leave his country, family, and father's house.

Abram allowed God to lead him to a destination he did not know (Canaan, which later became known as Israel, the promised land). Abram pressed through with every mile he walked in sandstorms, heat, and maybe much hardship. When he walked that desert land, he believed God had a good plan and that it was God's job to figure out how to bring it to pass. Abram's job was to follow God. As God told Abram to turn left or right or go straight and stop, Abram trusted and obeyed Him. He wanted to please God and do His will.

God made a covenant (through circumcision) with Abram. He instructed Abram to walk before Him blamelessly and promised He would multiply him exceedingly. "Then Abram fell on his face, and God talked with him, saying: 'As for Me, behold, My covenant is with you, and you shall be a father of many nations. . . . I will make you exceedingly fruitful; and I will make nations of you, and kings shall come from you'" (Genesis 17:3-4, 6). At the time, his name was still Abram, and his wife, Sarah's, name was still Sarai, and God changed their names. "'No longer shall your name be called Abram, but your name shall be Abraham; for I have made you a father of many nations.' . . . Then God said to Abraham, 'As for Sarai your wife, you shall not call her name Sarai, but Sarah shall be her name. And I will bless her and also give you a son by her; then I will bless her, and she shall be a mother of nations; kings of peoples shall be from her'" (vv. 5, 15-16).

Let's look at another way that Abraham pursued God as he pressed through for breakthrough. "Now it came to pass after these things that God tested Abraham, and said to him, 'Abraham!' And he said, 'Here I am.' [God] said, 'Take now your son, your only son Isaac, whom you love, and go to the land of Moriah, and offer him there as a burnt offering on one of the mountains of which I shall tell you'" (Genesis 22:1-2). Abraham bound his son on the altar of wood "and Abraham stretched out his hand and took the knife to slay his son. But the Angel of the

Lord called to him from heaven and said, 'Abraham, Abraham!' So he said, 'Here I am.' And He said, 'Do not lay your hand on the lad, or do anything to him; for now I know that you fear God, since you have not withheld your son, your only son, from Me'" (vv. 10-12). Because Abraham obeyed God's voice, He said to Abraham, "I will bless you, and multiplying I will multiply your descendants as the stars of the heaven and as the sand which is on the seashore; and your descendants shall possess the gate of their enemies" (v. 17).

Abraham followed and obeyed God with every painful, agonizing, and heart-wrenching step up Mount Moriah to sacrifice his son Isaac whom God had promised to give to him many years earlier. Abraham was way out of his comfort zone; he pursued God, and he pressed through for breakthrough. Abraham knew that if the promise of being a father of many nations was to be fulfilled through his seed, it would be through his son Isaac. Abraham may have asked God why he had to do it that way, why require that type of obedience and pain from him, why there could not be a better or easier way to do what God wanted and get the results that He wanted. And Abraham may not have gotten an answer from God. Nonetheless, he obeyed God, believing that He would provide for Himself a lamb (in Isaac's place) as an offering—a sacrifice.

Abraham decided to pursue God even when in the natural realm it looked like God's plan did not make sense and Abraham would suffer the great loss of his son. But he knew his God would not lie to him or disappoint him. Abraham believed God, and the Word of God says, "It was accounted to him for righteousness" (Romans 4:3; Galatians 3:6). Abraham had to leave his carnal, or rational, mind behind. He had to let go of his thoughts, fears, opinions, heartbreak, and anger and trust God. He had to die to his own flesh and let God live through him. A death had to occur;

Abraham had to die to his will for the life of a nation (Israel). Israel had to be birthed through him and through his son Isaac and through Isaac's son Jacob.

Through this very testing of Abraham, the true beginning of his fathering spirit came forth. Before God could use Abraham to birth many nations, he had to trust God as his own Father. God chose to test Abraham in this way. Father God wanted Abraham to make the choice to relinquish his own rights and allow God to be God, his heavenly Father. If you will allow Him to be your heavenly Father, He will allow you to father and mother others as your spiritual children.

I believe in that moment when Abraham lifted up his knife to sacrifice his son Isaac all of heaven stopped in silence. God found faithfulness in Abraham. In one man's obedience, a nation was born, and the plan of redemption for all the people of the world was put in motion. Abraham experienced breakthrough by pressing into God.

God is not a dictator. He is a God of relationship and family. Dictators tell you what to do and are selfish in their desires. God gives you a free will and choice to follow Him, love Him, and be in relationship with Him. He wants relationship with you because He loves you; you are His child. Your Father God is not selfish. He is a giver. He gave His one and only Son, Jesus Christ, to die for you, so you could live forever and be in relationship with God your Father, Jesus, your Lord and Savior, and Holy Spirit, your counselor and friend. He gave, He gives, He gives. He is the giver of life.

He wants you to love Him and give your life to Him. You belong to Him; you are His child. He greatly misses His children when they are not in His family through salvation in His Son, Jesus Christ. He wants you to give Him your thoughts, ideas, opinions, judgments, anger, sadness, fears, anxieties, sickness, and more.

When you give these to Him, He is faithful to give you breakthrough of restoration, healing, hope, joy, new life, and so much more! He wants to bless you. He is faithful to bless your obedience in following Him. When you live in love, you live in God, and He lives in you! "This is how we know that we live in him and he in us: He has given us of his Spirit. And we have seen and testify that the Father has sent his Son to be the Savior of the world. If anyone acknowledges that Jesus is the Son of God, God lives in them and they in God. And so we know and rely on the love God has for us. God is love. Whoever lives in love lives in God, and God in them" (1 John 4:13–16 NIV).

Ask yourself:

— Do I know that as one man, one woman, or one child, my obedience to God can affect a family, a city, a nation, and more?

— Am I willing today to give God my plans, my vision, and my desires so His plans, vision, and desires will come forth in my life, those lives I am praying for, and those lives I will impact?

Abraham completely trusted God with what he loved (his son Isaac) without knowing or understanding the reasons or outcome of what God asked him to do. Abraham pursued God as he pressed through for breakthrough.

— 12 —

When Kings, Judges, and Prophets Press Through

2 CHRONICLES 20:17

Take up your positions; stand firm and see the deliverance the Lord will give you.

God is very pleased when you pursue Him and allow His pressing process upon your life. Both King Jehosophat and judge and prophetess Deborah pursued God as they pressed through for breakthrough.

JEHOSHAPHAT

King Jehoshaphat pursued God as he pressed through for breakthrough.

King Jehoshaphat was a good king. He was told that a vast army of Moabites, Ammonites, and some of the Meunites was coming against the people of Judah and Jerusalem. This same army was an enemy to them in the past, and though the Israelites had wanted to invade this enemy's territory, the Lord would not allow them to do it at that time. Now the same three enemy armies were trying to drive the Israelites from the land the Lord God gave to them. "Alarmed, Jehoshaphat resolved to inquire of the Lord, and he proclaimed a fast for all Judah. The people of Judah came together to seek help from the Lord; indeed, they came from every town in Judah to seek him" (2 Chronicles 20:3-4 NIV). They asked the Lord for His help to overcome them. "Our God, will you not judge them? For we have no power to face this vast army that is attacking us. We do not know what to do, but our eyes are on you" (v. 12).

King Jehoshaphat pursued the Lord to learn His plan. When he did, the prophet Jahaziel spoke on behalf of God Almighty, and God told them that the battle was not theirs but His to fight. They pursued the Lord God in their faith and listened. They believed He wanted to help them and that He had the most excellent plan for them. He did! He said, "Tomorrow march down against them. They will be climbing up by the Pass of Ziz, and you will find them at the end of the gorge in the Desert of Jeruel. You will not have to fight this battle. Take up your positions; stand firm and see the deliverance the Lord will give you, Judah and Jerusalem. Do not be afraid; do not be discouraged. Go out to face them tomorrow, and the Lord will be with you.'" (vv. 16-17). They chose to do His will and they experienced the breakthrough and won the battle! The Lord gave them victory by causing the three enemy armies to destroy each other. Then, God enabled them to plunder the enemy and take "equipment and clothing and also articles of value—more than they could take away. There was so much plunder that it took three days to collect it" (v. 25). "The fear of God came on all the surrounding kingdoms when they heard how the Lord had fought against the enemies of Israel. And the kingdom of Jehoshaphat was at peace, for his God had given him rest on every side" (vv. 29-30).

It must have taken great courage for Judah and Jerusalem to go out before the enemy armies knowing that God told them they were not to fight the enemy. They had to believe that God would do what He said He would do, that He would fight for them. They knew that they just needed to follow His instructions, have faith, seek His will, pursue Him, listen to Him, trust and obey Him, and do His will with every step they took.

King Jehoshaphat pursued God as he pressed through for breakthrough.

Deborah

Deborah, judge and prophetess of Israel, pursued God as she pressed through for breakthrough.

When Deborah was prophetess and judge, the children of Israel did evil in the sight of the Lord. The Lord sold them to Jabin, King of Canaan, and he oppressed them harshly for twenty years.

> Now Deborah, a prophetess, the wife of Lapidoth, was judging Israel at that time. ... She sent and called for Barak the son of Abinoam from Kedesh in Naphtali, and said to him, "Has not the Lord God of Israel commanded, 'Go and deploy troops at Mount Tabor; take with you ten thousand men of the sons of Naphtali and of the sons of Zebulun; and against you I will deploy Sisera, the commander of Jabin's army, with his chariots and his multitude at the River Kishon; and I will deliver him into your hand'?"
>
> — Judges 4:4, 6-7

Barak said he would only go if Deborah went with him, and because of it, Deborah told Barak that she would, but there would be no glory for him in the journey because the Lord would "sell Sisera into the hand of a woman" (v. 9) instead of Barak. "And the Lord routed Sisera and all his chariots and all his army with the edge of the sword before Barak; and Sisera alighted from his chariot and fled away on foot. But Barak pursued the chariots and the army . . . and all the army of Sisera fell by the edge of the sword; not a man was left. However, Sisera had fled away on foot to the tent of Jael, the wife of Heber the Kenite" (vv. 15–17).

Sisera hid in Jael's tent. She covered him with a blanket, waited until he was asleep, and then drove a tent peg into his temple, and he died. When Barak arrived at Jael's tent, she showed him Sisera's dead body. "So on that day God subdued Jabin king of Canaan in the presence of the children of Israel. And the hand of the children of Israel grew stronger and stronger against Jabin king of Canaan, until they had destroyed Jabin king of Canaan" (vv. 23–24).

> Then Deborah and Barak the son of Abinoam sang on that day, saying: "When leaders lead in Israel, when the people willingly offer themselves, bless the Lord!" Hear, O kings! Give ear, O princes! I, even I, will sing to the Lord; I will sing praise to the Lord God of Israel. . . . So the land had rest for forty years."
>
> — Judges 5:1–3, 31

Dear reader, the Lord your God is your breaker! He will go before you in battle. He breaks down and through the strongholds of the enemy opposing you in your life. Cry out to Him, and He will answer you and give you breakthrough! Break out in song and sing praises to the Lord for the breakthrough He has given to you and is about to give you! Praise Him for His goodness and faithfulness to you! You have a song in your spirit, a song of breakthrough and victory! Come and break out in song to the Lord with praise!

Deborah pursued God as she pressed through for breakthrough. She had complete faith and knew God had a plan to destroy Israel's enemies—nations who had held them in cruel bondage for twenty years. There was not a doubt in her mind that He would give her people breakthrough! She was steadfast, she knew the Lord's voice, and she prophesied what He told her to the king on behalf of the Israelites and His love for them. She knew it was vitally important for her, and them, to have faith in God, seek God, listen to Him, trust and obey Him, do His will, and follow Him at all costs, no matter what the circumstances looked like and felt like.

Ask yourself:

- Is God asking me to climb a mountain in obedience, like Abraham did? Jesus did this for all mankind. He climbed Golgotha's hill to follow His Father's will so all humanity could be saved and live with Him forever.
- Have I ever felt that God has, or is, asking me to do something that is beyond my comprehension, abilities, level of comfort, and patience?
- Have I felt, or do I feel, that He is asking the impossible of me?

God is your faithful Father who will not test you beyond what you can handle. I encourage you to press through for breakthrough by pursuing God.

MY OWN STORY

Here is a personal example of how I pursued God and pressed through for breakthrough.

My husband and I tried to conceive a child for a year or so, but we had not been able to. I wanted to be a mother more than anything in the world. We were so elated and excited when we found out that I was pregnant with our first child. The doctor wanted to do the first sonogram at six weeks, so I set it early for the following Monday, even though I had planned on setting it that following Friday. On Saturday, while we were walking in the mall, I felt pain on my right lower abdomen come and go frequently. At my appointment two days later, I was told I had an ectopic pregnancy in my right fallopian tube.

The doctor told me he had to get me into emergency surgery to remove my fallopian tube at the hospital across the street, but it was not on my insurance plan. So I asked the doctor if we could go to mine across town, but he said they didn't have time. I was told that a female's fallopian tube is the width of a dry vermicelli noodle, and mine was the size of a cooked hot dog and was ready to burst. Later, I learned that an ectopic pregnancy is among the six most dangerous, life-threatening diagnoses a person can have, included with having a massive heart attack or a stroke. The doctor said that the baby had attached itself to my fallopian tube, but it should have been in my uterus. Determined to save my baby, I said to him, "We need to pray that the baby will move from the fallopian tube into my uterus." He said, "It will not move, and we need to remove your tube right away." With panic, shock, and sorrow, I realized they were going to take my baby from me! My mind was racing. *There has to be some way to save my baby. They cannot take my baby!*

I asked my husband to call our friend who was a nurse to get her advice. She said, "Liz, I was just going out the door, and I heard the phone ring. You have to do what the doctors are telling you and go into emergency surgery *now.*" Crying, I said okay, because I trusted her and trusted that she heard from God.

The doctor's nurse came in and led me to a tiny changing room to put on a surgery gown because they needed to wheel me across the street to the hospital right away. I was sobbing and crying out to God. "Why is this happening? I want to save my baby!" But I knew I could not, the doctors could not, and God was not going to. I told Him, "This hurts so deeply." He said to my heart, *I know, and I am hurting with you.* Then I heard Him say, *This is a victory.* I did not understand that—it did not make sense to me, and I could not process it. I just believed Him and trusted Him. Though I was filled with heartache, I felt God's presence, love, and comfort envelop me in such a special way at this time. Because of this conversation with Him, I named our baby Victoria. I did not know if our baby was a girl or a boy, but I sensed it was a girl. Later I thought *If our baby is a boy, his name will be Victor.* So at that moment in the changing room, I talked with my baby and said, "I love you very much, and I'm so sorry."

I was in shock and that is all I remember of that day. I do not remember being wheeled on the bed across the street to the hospital or going into the emergency room. I do not remember leaving the hospital or coming home after the surgery. I just remember lying in bed at home and going into a deep depression that lasted a few weeks.

I had to continue working full time at my job and serving in my church with my husband as a deacon. I felt alone and carried a deep loss. People did not know what to say, and I felt alone in this with God and my husband. Then, a few weeks later, my pastors asked me to become the director of the children's department at church. I was offended and thought it was insensitive of them to ask me this since I had just lost my baby. I thought they should know how difficult it would be for me to be around babies and children at this time. But I told them I would pray about it. I prayed and felt the Lord press upon me that He wanted me to do this. As I look back, I think my pastors may have thought this would help me to heal. I decided to follow the Lord and accept this new assignment and told my pastors I would. They were so happy. With some heaviness, I went in my first day, saw the children, and fell in love with them right away. The healing process of my heartache began immediately and continued over the next few weeks, and I had much joy in serving these little ones and their parents!

"How Can This Be a Victory?"

As I recovered, I asked God how this great loss of our baby could be a victory. He gave me partial understanding when I felt Him say, *It is a victory because your life was spared.*

I understood this with my mind, but I did not understand in my heart why my life was spared and my baby's was not. I looked back at the events leading up to the sonogram appointment and realized if I had not made the appointment for the sonogram on Monday but waited until later in the week on Friday, my fallopian tube could have burst when I was not close to a hospital. God could have made a way for me to be near a hospital, but for reasons I do not know, He chose for me to go through this challenge in this way. Though I do not understand why all of this happened, I believe I will know when I am in heaven. I rest in knowing that God in His wisdom, love, and mercy knows what He is doing, He is in charge, and I need to trust Him.

When I had the ectopic pregnancy, I did not have the choice to keep my baby. It was beyond my control, but I did have the choice to continue to follow God and be devoted to Him after my loss. I chose to follow Him, and I received healing, growth, and joy that I would not have had if I did not follow Him. I had to press through for breakthrough by pursuing Him.

After the ectopic pregnancy, my husband and I tried for three more years to conceive a child, but we could not. One day, during these three years, I was reading the Bible and heard in my spirit, *Your son's name shall be called Nathanael.* It was such a soft, gentle, matter-of-fact voice, and it settled in my spirit. I responded, "Oh, okay, I guess we are going to have a boy," and I continued reading. Then, three days later while my husband and I were in church, my husband turned to me and quietly said, "Liz, I just heard God say, *"Your son's name shall be called Nathanael."* I looked amazed at him and said, "He told me that three days ago! We are going to have a boy!" We were so happy, while trying to not make any noise.

We held on to this truth from God that we would one day have a son. Toward the end of these three years of trying to get pregnant, we went to the doctor, and he said that my husband and I would each need tests done to see why I had not become pregnant. The tests showed that each of us had physical limitations to me getting pregnant, and one of mine was that I now only had one fallopian tube from the ectopic pregnancy surgery three years earlier. The doctor said there were some procedures we could each do that might help, so we had them done. The doctor also said for me to have a light work schedule, so I changed my job to one that had less pressure and was only five minutes from home.

Then, within a couple of months, I got pregnant! We were so excited and told our families that we were going to have a boy and that his name would be Nathanael. This gave us an opportunity to witness to our families and others about how God shared this good news with us about our son. Our families were happy for us but perplexed as to how we could know the baby's gender and already have a name for him. I asked God, "Will this baby come to full term and not be another ectopic pregnancy?" I felt He said, *He is firmly planted in your womb and he will be born full term.* Eight months later, our son Nathanael was born, and what a joy he was and has been—for twenty-two years now!

When I was seven months pregnant with Nathanael, one night I had sudden, very heavy pain in my back that made it difficult to breathe, talk, and stand up straight. This was before we had cell phones, and my husband had just left the house to go exercise at the YMCA a few blocks away. With difficulty breathing, I desperately called the YMCA and told them to have my husband call me as soon as he got there. He came home quickly. He laid hands on me and prayed for the pain to go, and suddenly, it went away. I went to the doctor the next day, and he told me that I had gallstones. He said they commonly develop during pregnancy and that if I had another episode like this, I would need surgery to remove my gallbladder. This was scary to hear. Though the surgery could be done when seven months pregnant, the recovery would be quite difficult and very uncomfortable in the third trimester of pregnancy. We prayed for my healing, and I did not have any more episodes of this type of pain during pregnancy. But when our son was about two months old, I had a very painful episode again, went to the emergency room, and had my gallbladder removed.

During these trials of an ectopic pregnancy, not getting pregnant for a few years, having a very intense episode of gallbladder pain, and potentially needing surgery while pregnant, I chose to:

1. Have faith and believe that God loves me, wants a relationship with me, and has a great plan for my life;
2. Seek God's will;
3. Listen to God;
4. Trust God, obey Him, wait on Him, and believe that He would bring me breakthrough;
5. Do God's will at all costs, no matter what the circumstances look like or feel like.

God wanted me to pursue Him, follow His will, press into Him (lean on Him and trust in Him), and allow His pressing process upon my life so His rich oil could come through my life to bless me, Him, and others.

When you press into the Lord your God and you feel His pressing process upon your life, lean on Him and trust in Him. He is always with you; you are never alone. He so wants you to talk with Him about the minutest details and your needs. He wants to help you to hear the loving and encouraging words He speaks to you. He is your burden bearer, and He helps you to stay close to Him. He is your breaker, comforter, provider, protector, and deliverer; and He wants you to be fulfilled, joyful, and free. As you live for Him and follow Him, you will have breakthrough!

God wants you to pursue Him with all your heart. As God's presses upon your life occur, He helps you to press into Him and know that He is faithful to bring you breakthrough. God has a great vision, plan, and outcome for your life that will not only affect you but your family and many other people's lives too. Are you willing to make the sacrifice and pursue Him for breakthrough?

Ask yourself:

— Can I take a few moments and write about a time when I pursued God as I pressed through for breakthrough?

— Am I in a difficult situation now, when I need to pursue God and press through to receive my breakthrough?

— Can I think of some people in the Bible I would like to study regarding how they pursued God as they pressed through for breakthrough?

MY COMMITMENT

I (put your name here) pursued God as I pressed through or am pressing through for breakthrough.

God wants me to pursue Him, follow His will, press in, and allow His pressing process upon my life, so His rich oil can come through my life to bless me, God, and others.

I (_____) chose to or I choose to:

1. Have faith and believe that God loves me, wants a relationship with me, and has a great plan for my life;
2. Seek God's will;
3. Listen to God;
4. Trust God, obey Him, wait on Him, and believe that He will bring me breakthrough;
5. Do God's will at all costs, no matter what the circumstances look like or feel like.

THOUGHTS

THOUGHTS

Thoughts

Note from Liz

And so, dear reader, we come to the end of this guidebook on how to press through for your breakthrough. Jesus teaches you how to press through for breakthrough in difficult times. He knew that when He submitted Himself to His Father's pressing process, it would result in great blessing for many. He trusted Father God through it all, and so can you.

God has already anointed you for breakthrough with His abundance, empowerment, consecration, healing, and joy. Surrendering to His will and pressing through will keep you in the anointing He so willingly provides. No one is more zealous about your breakthrough and your healing than your Father. He will preserve you, and He is faithful to stay with you at all times.

Jesus is the breaker—He has broken every chain, and as you walk with Him and in His authority and truth, He will bring you breakthrough. Just as He walked with, guided, and provided for the Israelites in the desert for forty years, He will walk with, guide, and provide for you. He has already sacrificed everything for you, and His heart never changes.

It can be difficult to find the hope and faith to pursue God when everything in life seems so hard, but He is the only place to run to, the only path to walk on. In Him is all you need. You can rest your thoughts, your body, and your emotions in Him as you pray, worship, and receive healing. When you completely surrender to His ways, spend a lot of time in His presence, and let Holy Spirit guide you in all your ways, you will find yourself becoming more and more like Jesus. The more intimate you are with Him, the more aware you will be of anything in your life that is not aligned with His heart, and you will be ready to receive His strength in all the areas where you are weak.

Note from Liz

The way the Lord Jesus Christ, Bible heroes, kings, judges, and prophets pressed through for their breakthroughs gives you hope and inspires you to imitate their faith and trust in the Lord. May your breakthrough be like theirs, so that when you come through it all your heart and soul will have gone wider, longer, higher, and deeper in God's love, and you will overflow with the wisdom, faith, and blessings you have gained in your journey with Him.

For this reason I bow my knees to the Father of our Lord Jesus Christ, from whom the whole family in heaven and earth is named, that He would grant you, according to the riches of His glory, to be strengthened with might through His Spirit in the inner man, that Christ may dwell in your hearts through faith; that you, being rooted and grounded in love, may be able to comprehend with all the saints what is the width and length and depth and height—to know the love of Christ which passes knowledge; that you may be filled with all the fullness of God.

— Ephesians 3:14–19

Dear reader, if you have not yet received salvation from sin that Jesus Christ freely gives to you, please consider receiving Him as your Lord and Savior today. He loves you so much and wants you to receive His and Father God's love. The apostle John put it this way: "This is how God showed his love among us: He sent his one and only Son into the world that we might live through him. This is love: not that we loved God, but that he loved us and sent his Son as an atoning sacrifice for our sins" (1 John 4:9–10 NIV).

Salvation in Jesus Christ

Sin separates you from God. Sin is choosing your way instead of God's way of living. God has a better life-giving and more fulfilling way for you to live. Sin leads to death, but God wants you to have eternal life with Him. So He sent His Son, Jesus, to die for your sins and give you eternal life with Him! Jesus Christ came to earth, shed His blood, and died on the cross to save you from your sins. And then God, His Father, raised him from death to life. Father God so wants you to have relationship with Him and be in His family. He wants you to receive Jesus as your Lord and Savior and ask Him each day to help you to follow Him. Jesus loves you, and He forgives you of your sins. He so desires to help you every step of the way, and He wants a close relationship with you, for He loves you with an everlasting love! "The Lord has appeared of old to me, saying: 'Yes, I have loved you with an everlasting love; therefore, with lovingkindness I have drawn you'" (Jeremiah 31:3).

Would you like to receive Jesus Christ as your Lord and Savior? If you would, follow the ABCs of salvation through Jesus Christ, listed below:

— **ADMIT** to God that you are a sinner. Repent, turn away from your sin, and ask God to forgive you for your sins. Accept Jesus Christ as your Lord and Savior.

— **BELIEVE** that Jesus Christ is God's only begotten Son and that Jesus came to save mankind from eternal death and give mankind eternal life. When you believe in Jesus as your Savior and Lord, He forgives you of your sins.

— **CONFESS** your faith in Jesus Christ as your Savior and Lord.

Dear child of God, congratulations, you are saved! Jesus Christ, your Savior and Lord intercedes for you—He prays for you. Nothing shall ever separate you from His everlasting love for you. Welcome to God's family!

NOTE FROM LIZ

Listed in Appendix G on page 176 are Scriptures for the ABCs of salvation, so you can learn more about God's plan of salvation and His love for you.

Liz

APPENDIX A

CHARACTERISTICS OF FAITH

Characteristics of faith that God gives to you for breakthrough as you press in to know Him and live for Him.

You cannot see faith, yet it is a substance. (Hebrews 11:1)
It is impossible to please God without faith. (Hebrews 11:6)
Faith purifies your heart. (Acts 15:8–9)
Faith is a good fight. (1 Timothy 6:12)
God is faithful. (2 Timothy 2:13 NIV)
Faith is full of assurance. (Hebrews 10:22)
You are established in faith. (Colossians 2:6–7)
Faith is a breastplate. (1 Thessalonians 5:8)
Faith is a shield. (Ephesians 6:16)
Faith came by way of Jesus. (Galatians 3:25 NLT)
You are sons of God through faith in Christ Jesus. (Galatians 3:26–29 NIV)
Faith grows. (2 Thessalonians 1:3 NIV)
Faith works by love. (Galatians 5:6 NIV)
You are of the household of faith. (Galatians 6:9–10)
Faith keeps you grounded. (Colossians 1:21–23)
You serve with faith. (Philippians 2:17 NIV)
Faith edifies. (1 Timothy 1:3–7)
You are saved through faith. (Ephesians 2:8 NIV)
With your faith you have a pure conscience (refers to deacons, but good for all believers as well). (1 Timothy 3:9 NIV)
You can have bold faith. (1 Timothy 3:13)
You can deny faith. (1 Timothy 5:8)

You can depart from faith. (1 Timothy 4:1–5)

You can lack in faith. (1 Thessalonians 3:10 NIV)

You can have abundant faith. (1 Timothy 1:14)

You must contend for faith. (Jude 1:3)

Faith justifies you. (Romans 3:28; Galatians 2:16; 3:8, 11, 24 NIV)

(NKJV: "The Just") (NIV: "The Righteous") shall live by faith. (Galatians 3:11–12)

Faith gives righteousness. (Romans 9:30 NIV)

Faith is the opposite of sin. (Romans 14:19–23 NIV)

Faith enables you to stand firm. (2 Corinthians 1:21–24; 1 Corinthians 16:13 NIV)

Faith is an operation of God. (Colossians 2:12)

Faith is a work. (1 Thessalonians 1:3; James 2:18–26)

Your faith will be tried. (1 Peter 1:7 KJV)

Through faith, you can subdue kingdoms. (Hebrews 11:32–35)

APPENDIX B

The Hall of Faith, Hebrews 11

By faith we understand. (Hebrews 11:1–3)

Faith at the dawn of history (vv. 4–7)

Faithful Abraham (vv. 8–12)

The heavenly hope (vv. 13–16)

The faith of the patriarchs (vv. 17–22)

The faith of Moses (vv. 23–29)

By faith they overcame. (vv. 30–40)

APPENDIX C

PRAYING TO FATHER GOD, JESUS, AND HOLY SPIRIT

I suggest the following articles:

- "Should I Pray to the Father, the Son, or the Spirit?" by John Piper
- https://www.desiringgod.org/interviews/should-i-pray-to-the-father-the-son-or-the-spirit
- "Should we only pray to the Father as Jesus Taught? Or Is It Okay to Pray to Jesus and the Spirit?" by Shari Abbott
- https://reasonsforhopejesus.com/only-pray-to-the-father

APPENDIX D

For definitions and Scripture references on the difference between prayer, supplication, petition, and intercession, please see The Living Word Library Christian Resource Centre.

www.wordlibrary.co.uk/article.php?id=590

APPENDIX E

What only Jesus could do

- ✓ Serve and give His life as a ransom for many (Matthew 20:28)
- ✓ Taste death for everyone (Hebrews 2:9)
- ✓ Die and destroy Satan who held the power of death (Hebrews 2:14)
- ✓ Destroy the devil's works (1 John 3:8)
- ✓ Become a merciful and high priest to make atonement for the sins of the people (Hebrews 2:17)
- ✓ Take away your sin (1 John 3:5 NIV)
- ✓ Reunite you to Father God (John 14:6)
- ✓ Save the world (John 3:17 NIV)
- ✓ Save you, give you life abundantly and eternal life (John 10:9–10, 27–28)
- ✓ Be the first to preach the good news of the kingdom of God (Luke 4:43 NIV)
- ✓ Come down from heaven to do the will of Father God (John 6:38 NIV)
- ✓ Give Father God's words (John 17:8 NIV)
- ✓ Reveal Father God to those Jesus chooses to reveal Him (Matthew 11:27 NIV)
- ✓ Testify to the truth (John 18:37)
- ✓ Fulfill the Law and the Prophets (Matthew 5:17)
- ✓ Preach, proclaim, recover, and set free (Luke 4:18–19; Matthew 11:4–5 NIV)

- ✓ Bring judgment (John 9:39 NIV)
- ✓ Call sinners to repentance (Luke 5:31–32 NIV)
- ✓ Give understanding (1 John 5:20 NIV)
- ✓ Have keys of Hades and of death (Revelation 1:18)

APPENDIX F

My Identity in Jesus Christ

"I AM" AFFIRMATIONS

New King James Version (NKJV) unless otherwise noted

IN CHRIST:

- ✓ I am born again of the Spirit. (John 3:6–7)
- ✓ I am crucified with Christ, nevertheless I live. (Galatians 2:20)
- ✓ I am a new creation; the old has passed away. (2 Corinthians 5:17)
- ✓ I am dead, and my life is hidden with Christ in God. (Colossians 3:3)
- ✓ I am a new person created to be like God in true righteousness and holiness. (Ephesians 4:24; Colossians 3:9–11)
- ✓ I live and move and have my being in Christ. (Acts 17:28)
- ✓ I am a slave to righteousness: I am not a slave to sin. (Romans 6:18; 2 Corinthians 5:21)
- ✓ I am crucified to the world, and I have overcome the world. (Galatians 6:14; 1 John 5:4)
- ✓ I have eternal life. (John 3:14–15, Romans 6:23)
- ✓ I am the salt of the earth. (Matthew 5:13)
- ✓ I am the light of the world. (Matthew 5:14)
- ✓ I bear much fruit, and my fruit remains. (John 15:5, 8, 16)
- ✓ I abide in God's love. (John 15:9–10)

APPENDICES

- ✓ I am full of joy. (John 15:11; 17:13; Psalm 16:11)
- ✓ I am God's friend. (John 15:14-15)
- ✓ I am chosen and appointed by God. (John 15:16)
- ✓ I have an effective prayer life. (James 5:16)
- ✓ I am in the Father and the Son, and they are in me. (John 17:21-23)
- ✓ I am filled with the love of God. (John 17:26)
- ✓ I have peace with God. (Romans 5:1; Ephesians 2:14; Colossians 1:20)
- ✓ I am justified, and I am no longer under condemnation. (Romans 5:9; 8:1-2; Galatians 2:16)
- ✓ I am a son of God, and I can cry out, "Abba! Father!" (Romans 8:15; Galatians 4:6)
- ✓ I am not a slave to fear. (Romans 8:15)
- ✓ I am joint heir with Christ as a child of God. (Romans 8:17; Galatians 3:29)
- ✓ I am being transformed by the renewing of my mind. (Romans 12:2)
- ✓ I am more than a conqueror through Christ. (Romans 8:37)
- ✓ I have a new mind, the mind of Christ. (Ephesians 4:23; 1 Corinthians 2:16)
- ✓ I am one spirit with the Lord. (1 Corinthians 6:17)
- ✓ I am the temple of the Holy Spirit, and I have been bought with a price. (1 Corinthians 3:16; 6:19-20)
- ✓ I am reconciled to God. (2 Corinthians 5:18-19; Colossians 1:22)
- ✓ I am an ambassador for Christ. (2 Corinthians 5:20)

APPENDICES

- ✓ I am the righteousness of God in Jesus Christ. (2 Corinthians 5:21)
- ✓ I am delivered out of this present evil age. (Galatians 1:4)
- ✓ I have the blessing of Abraham, the promise of the Spirit. (Galatians 3:14)
- ✓ I am clothed with Christ. (Galatians 3:27 NIV)
- ✓ I am a saint and faithful in Christ Jesus. (Ephesians 1:1; Colossians 1:2)
- ✓ I am blessed with every spiritual blessing. (Ephesians 1:3)
- ✓ I was chosen in Christ before the foundation of the world. (Ephesians 1:4)
- ✓ I am chosen to be holy and without blame. (Ephesians 1:4)
- ✓ I was predestined by God to be adopted as a son. (Ephesians 1:5)
- ✓ I have been redeemed and forgiven of my trespasses through His blood because of the riches of His grace, which He has lavished upon me. (Ephesians 1:7-8; Colossians 1:13–14)
- ✓ I am sealed with the Holy Spirit of promise. (Ephesians 1:13)
- ✓ I am God's own possession. (Ephesians 1:14 NIV)
- ✓ I am loved with God's great love. (Ephesians 2:4)
- ✓ I am alive in Christ and have been raised with Him and seated with Him in the heavenly places. (Ephesians 2:5-6)
- ✓ I am saved by grace. It is the gift of God. (Ephesians 2:8)
- ✓ I am His workmanship, created for good works. (Ephesians 2:10)
- ✓ I have access to the Father through the Spirit. (Ephesians 2:18)

- ✓ I have been brought near by the blood of Christ. (Ephesians 2:13; Hebrews 10:19–22)
- ✓ I am no longer a stranger and foreigner, but I am a fellow citizen with the saints and a member of the household of God. (Ephesians 2:19)
- ✓ Along with all the saints, I am being fitted together into a holy temple in the Lord and being built for a dwelling place (as a spiritual house) of God in the Spirit. (Ephesians 2:22; 1 Peter 2:5)
- ✓ I have bold and confident access to God. (Ephesians 3:12; Hebrews 4:16)
- ✓ I am strengthened with power through His Spirit in my inner man. (Ephesians 3:16; Colossians 1:29 NIV)
- ✓ I am growing up in all aspects into Christ. (Ephesians 4:5)
- ✓ I am an imitator of Christ; I walk in love. (Ephesians 5:1-2)
- ✓ I am a child of light, I do not walk in darkness. (Ephesians 5:8; 1 Thessalonians 5:5)
- ✓ I am strong in the Lord and in the strength of His might. (Ephesians 6:10)
- ✓ I am being poured out as a drink offering. (Philippians 2:17)
- ✓ I am of the circumcision. . . . I worship God in the Spirit. . . . I rejoice in Christ Jesus. . . . I have no confidence in the flesh. (Philippians 3:3)
- ✓ I am pressing on toward the goal for the prize of the upward call of God in Christ Jesus. (Philippians 3:14)
- ✓ I am a citizen of heaven. (Philippians 3:20)

APPENDICES

- ✓ My heart and my mind are guarded by the peace of God. (Philippians 4:7)
- ✓ I can do all things through Christ who strengthens me. (Philippians 4:13)
- ✓ My needs are supplied by my God according to His riches in glory by Christ Jesus. (Philippians 4:19)
- ✓ I have been rescued from the dominion of darkness, and brought into the kingdom of His beloved Son. (Colossians 1:13)
- ✓ I am rooted in Him. (Colossians 2:7)
- ✓ I am built up in Him. (Colossians 2:7)
- ✓ I am complete in Him. (Colossians 2:10)
- ✓ I have been buried with Him in baptism, raised up with Him through faith and made alive with Him. (Colossians 2:12-13)
- ✓ I am growing with the increase that is from God. (Colossians 2:19)
- ✓ I am dead to the elemental spiritual forces of the world. (Colossians 2:20 NIV)
- ✓ I am chosen of God, holy and dearly loved. (Colossians 3:12; 1 Thessalonians 1:4 NIV)
- ✓ I am saved from wrath through Him. (Romans 5:9)
- ✓ I have been given a spirit of power and love and sound mind. (2 Timothy 1:7)
- ✓ I have been called by God to a holy calling. (2 Timothy 1:9; Hebrews 3:1)
- ✓ I am strong in the grace that is in Christ Jesus. (2 Timothy 2:1)

- ✓ I am a partaker of Christ of His divine nature. (Hebrews 3:14; 2 Peter 1:4)
- ✓ I have confidence to enter the Most Holy Place by the blood of Jesus. (Hebrews 10:19 NIV)
- ✓ I am of a chosen generation, a royal priesthood, a holy nation, His own special people. (1 Peter 2:9)
- ✓ I am in Him who is true, in His Son Jesus Christ. (1 John 5:20)

APPENDIX G

Scriptures for salvation

ADMIT to God that you are a sinner. Repent, turn away from your sin, and ask God to forgive you for your sins. Accept Jesus Christ as your Savior and Lord.

- All of mankind has sinned.

"For all have sinned and fall short of the glory of God." (Romans 3:23).

- Sin separates you from God.

"But your iniquities have separated you from your God; And your sins have hidden His face from you, so that He will not hear." (Isaiah 59:2).

- Sin leads to death.

"For the wages of sin is death, but the gift of God is eternal life in Christ Jesus our Lord." (Romans 6:23)

- Repent and be converted so that your sins will be removed.

"Repent therefore and be converted, that your sins may be blotted out, so that times of refreshing may come from the presence of the Lord." (Acts 3:19)

BELIEVE that Jesus Christ is God's only begotten Son and that Jesus came to save mankind from their sins and death and give mankind eternal life. When you believe in Jesus as your Savior and Lord, He forgives you of your sins.

- Jesus, the Son of Man ascended into heaven. Whoever believes in Him will have everlasting life and be saved.

"No one has ascended to heaven but He who came down from heaven, that is, the Son of Man who is in heaven. And as Moses lifted up the serpent in the wilderness, even so must the Son of Man be lifted up, that whoever believes in Him should not perish but have eternal life. For God so loved the world that He gave His only begotten Son, that whoever believes in Him should not perish but have everlasting life. For God did not send His Son into the world to condemn the world, but that the world through Him might be saved." (John 3:13–17)

"So they said, 'Believe on the Lord Jesus Christ, and you will be saved, you and your household.'" (Acts 16:31)

- You are saved through your faith in Jesus Christ.

"For by grace you have been saved through faith, and that not of yourselves; it is the gift of God, not of works, lest anyone should boast." (Ephesians 2:8–9)

- There is salvation for mankind only through Jesus Christ.

"Let it be known to you all, and to all the people of Israel, that by the name of Jesus Christ of Nazareth, whom you crucified, whom God raised from the dead, by Him this man stands here before you whole. This is the 'stone which was rejected by you builders, which has become the chief cornerstone.' Nor is there salvation in any other, for there is no other name under heaven given among men by which we must be saved." (Acts 4:10–12)

- God sent Jesus, His only Begotten Son, so that you might live through Him.

"In this the love of God was manifested toward us, that God has sent His only begotten Son into the world, that we might live through Him." (1 John 4:9)

- Jesus is the only way to come to Father God—to be reconciled to Him

"Jesus said to him, 'I am the way, the truth, and the life. No one comes to the Father except through Me.'" (John 14:6)

- Believe that Christ died for you as a sinner and reconciled you to Him. He saves you from death.

"But God demonstrates His own love toward us, in that while we were still sinners, Christ died for us. Much more then, having now been justified by His blood, we shall be saved from wrath through Him. For if when we were enemies we were reconciled to God through the death of His Son, much more, having been reconciled, we shall be saved by His life. And not only that, but we also rejoice in God through our Lord Jesus Christ, through whom we have now received the reconciliation." (Romans 5:8–11)

- Those who receive Jesus as their Savior and Lord are the children of God.

"He was in the world, and the world was made through Him, and the world did not know Him. He came to His own, and His own did not receive Him. But as many as received Him, to them He gave the right to become children of God, to those who believe in His name: who were born, not of blood, nor of the will of the flesh, nor of the will of man, but of God." (John 1:10–13)

- Jesus shed His blood (stripes from being stricken), and He took away your sins (iniquity) on the cross.

"But He was wounded for our transgressions, He was bruised for our iniquities; the chastisement for our peace was upon Him, and by His stripes we are healed. All we like sheep have gone astray; we have turned, every one, to his own way; and the Lord has laid on Him the iniquity of us all." (Isaiah 53:5–6)

- Jesus died and rose from death and lived again.

"They will scourge Him and kill Him. And the third day He will rise again." (Luke 18:33)

"For to this end Christ died and rose and lived again, that He might be Lord of both the dead and the living." (Romans 14:9)

"That Christ died for our sins according to the Scriptures, and that He was buried, and that He rose again the third day according to the Scriptures." (1 Corinthians 15:3-4)

- Jesus will come back to earth again.

"Let not your heart be troubled; you believe in God, believe also in Me. In My Father's house are many mansions; if it were not so, I would have told you. I go to prepare a place for you. And if I go and prepare a place for you, I will come again and receive you to Myself; that where I am, there you may be also. And where I go you know, and the way you know." (John 14:1-4)

CONFESS your faith in Jesus Christ as your Savior and Lord.

"If you confess with your mouth the Lord Jesus and believe in your heart that God has raised Him from the dead, you will be saved." (Romans 10:9)

"He who did not spare His own Son, but delivered Him up for us all, how shall He not with Him also freely give us all things? . . . It is Christ who died, and furthermore is also risen, who is even at the right hand of God, who also makes intercession for us. Who shall separate us from the love of Christ? Shall tribulation, or distress, or persecution, or famine, or nakedness, or peril, or sword? As it is written:

"'For Your sake we are killed all day long; we are accounted as sheep for the slaughter.' . . . Yet in all these things we are more than conquerors through Him who loved us. For I am persuaded that neither death nor life, nor angels nor principalities nor powers, nor things present nor things to come, nor height nor depth, nor any other created thing, shall be able to separate us from the love of God which is in Christ Jesus our Lord." (Romans 8:32, 34–39).

"Let your conduct be without covetousness; be content with such things as you have. For He Himself has said, 'I will never leave you nor forsake you.' So we may boldly say: 'The Lord is my helper; I will not fear. What can man do to me?'" (Hebrews 13:5–6)

About the Author

Liz Robinson is the cofounder and COO of WISE Ministries International and WISE Executive Coaching Solutions. An executive coach to CEOs and leaders in all sectors of society, she trains them how to thrive and succeed in their workplaces and as leaders. A teacher, life coach, pastoral counselor, and mentor, Liz ministers God's love and healing power with wisdom and spiritual insight.

Liz received her BS in Business Administration: Marketing from the University of Central Florida, completed training at Faith Theological Seminary and Christian College in Tampa, FL, and at Life Gate Church School of Ministry in Hurst, TX. With her husband, Charles, Liz co-pastored a vibrant church in Austin, Texas, for five years. Liz has twenty years of experience in ministering inner healing, fourteen years of experience in pastoral counseling and serving the local church, pastors, and communities, and to date has equipped more than 120 CEOs and business owners, many who serve those in Fortune 500 companies.

About the Author

Liz loves to intercede for people, communities, and nations. She loves to commune with the Lord, worship Him, study His Word, and receive His heart of love and wisdom for them.

When not ministering, Liz loves taking photographs, creating arts and crafts, bicycling, and walking in the mountains and by the ocean. She lives in Mission Viejo, California, with her husband and two dogs, Malty the Maltese and Penny Peanut.

Websites

WISE MINISTRIES INTERNATIONAL

Workplace. Intercession. Insight. Support. Empowerment.

www.coachmybusiness.com

WISE EXECUTIVE COACHING SOLUTIONS

www.wisecoaching.solutions

Contact Liz Robinson

For speaking engagements and coaching requests

E-MAIL: liz@coachmybusiness.com

CAN YOU HELP?

Reviews are everything to an author, because they mean a book is given more visibility. If you enjoyed this book, please review it on your favorite book review sites and tell your friends about it. Thank you!

www.ingramcontent.com/pod-product-compliance
Lightning Source LLC
Chambersburg PA
CBHW071202160426
43196CB00011B/2163